## Praise for *Big-Hearted Entrepreneur*

"If your heartfelt desire is to build a more human economy, driven by a sacred purpose, it's time to embrace Suzi Hunn's poignant message. In *Big-Hearted Entrepreneur* you'll find strategies to speak up, cultivate community, and send your stories into the world. As you tend the fire of resilience glowing within you, let Hunn's encouragement bring a candle of light."

**DR. TERERAI TRENT**, author of *The Awakened Woman*, educator, humanitarian, speaker, and Oprah Winfrey's favorite guest of all time

"Mission-centered entrepreneurs don't have to make a choice between being kind paupers or cold-blooded mercenaries. *Big-Hearted Entrepreneur* shows the way to purpose plus profit. With a clear drive to educate entrepreneurs on owning their worth, Suzi Hunn provides a refreshing, practical guide for newbies and veterans alike."

**JEFFREY DAVIS**, speaker, author, and CEO of Tracking Wonder

"For those transitioning from careers to entrepreneurship, this book is a must-have. Suzi Hunn's insights go beyond stories as she introduces reflections, application ideas, and actionable prompts, motivating readers to innovate and actualize their visions."

**SYBIL HALL**, founder of Well-Being & Wealth for Educators

"As an author and creative entrepreneur, Suzi Hunn puts forth thought leadership and positive practices that soothe my soul and move me to action—but without the pressure of the grind culture and without my doubting my own abilities. Combining info on money, mission, and mindset, *Big-Hearted Entrepreneur* is *the* book to get you where you want to go—in business and in life."
**BETHANY HEGEDUS**, award-winning author, founder and creative director of The Writing Barn and the Courage to Create community

"This beautifully crafted guide weaves together masterful storytelling, well-earned wisdoms, and immediate opportunities to discover new insights. I want every big-hearted entrepreneur I know (and the many I don't know, too!) to read this book!!! I am already rethinking some of my current practices, thanks to the loving, validating, and hopeful messages in this book. I can't wait to see where this inspiring journey takes me next!"
**SHONA RAMCHANDANI**, founder of the Chrysalis Consulting Collaborative

"*Big-Hearted Entrepreneur* is a guide that empowers us to infuse purpose and kindness into every aspect of our entrepreneurial endeavors. It offers a roadmap for building businesses that are not only financially viable but also contribute positively to the world around us. The insights and strategies shared are a source of inspiration for those of us who believe in the potential of business to create meaningful change."
**CINDY KARNES**, founder of the Empowered Hours Club

"*Big-Hearted Entrepreneur* is essential reading for those of us who are interested in changing the world... the radical changemakers, the passionate disrupters, those committed to making a joyful ruckus. Entrepreneurship is often a lonely venture of bringing forth your greatest gifts, but Suzi Hunn's book is a reminder that we are never in this work alone, and with her guidance and wisdom we can find our way to a more successful, whole, and connected version of ourselves and work."

**ERINN FARRELL**, co-founder of The Coven coworking community

"*Big-Hearted Entrepreneur* teaches you to let go of anything that keeps you small. This brave, honest book shares how to do deep work and empowers purpose-driven business leaders to improve the lives around them. Honest, inspiring, and helpful, this book is practical and shares meaningful, reflective practices on how to bring Hunn's lessons to life. I highly recommend it to anyone on a mission of caring in their business."

**AZUL TERRONEZ**, *Wall Street Journal-* and *USA Today-*bestselling author, TEDx speaker, and co-founder of Authors Who Lead

# Own Your Worth and Amplify a Mission That Matters

# BIG
# HEARTED
## ENTREPRENEUR

**Suzi Hunn**

● PAGE
● TWO

Copyright © 2023 by Suzi Hunn

All rights reserved. No part of this book may be reproduced, stored in a retrieval system or transmitted, in any form or by any means, without the prior written consent of the publisher, except in the case of brief quotations, embodied in reviews and articles.

Cataloguing in publication information is available from Library and Archives Canada.
978-1-77458-333-3 (paperback)
978-1-77458-339-5 (ebook)

Page Two
pagetwo.com

Edited by Kendra Ward
Copyedited by Madison Taylor
Cover, interior design, and
illustrations by Taysia Louie

teachyourthing.com

*To Kate: Since our teacher education days, you've floored me with your commitment to justice, education, and community. Together, let's spread the philosophy far and wide.*

*And to all the big-hearted entrepreneurs: May you live out your highest contribution.*

# Contents

**Calling All Loving Disruptors**
(A.K.A. Big-Hearted Entrepreneurs) *1*

PART ONE **OWN YOUR WORTH**

1. Get to Know Your Personal Medicine *15*
2. Be Profitable and Sustainable *27*
3. Power Up *37*
4. Leap! (A.K.A. Look for Lily Pads) *47*
5. Trust Your Inner Knowing *59*
6. Do Your Deep Work *69*
7. Protect Your Energy *77*
8. Make Time to Do the Most Good *87*
9. Choose Mission and Money *97*
10. Pay Attention to Your Wealth *109*

PART TWO **AMPLIFY A MISSION THAT MATTERS**

11 Embrace Authenticity over Perfection *127*

12 Facilitate Dialogue (A.K.A. Avoid the Loathsome Cliché) *137*

13 Cultivate Warm Connections *147*

14 Shout from the Rooftops *159*

15 Build a Body of Work *169*

16 Get Your Event On *179*

17 Develop a Signature Talk *189*

18 Teach Your Thing *201*

19 Propel Your People *211*

**Loving Disruptors,
May You Never Feel Alone** *221*

Acknowledgements *225*

Bibliography *227*

# Calling All Loving Disruptors

(A.K.A. Big-Hearted Entrepreneurs)

"Any entrepreneur who thinks they can change the world is fooling themselves. I've worked with hundreds of business owners, and the bottom line is all they care about." Here was Hollis, saying out loud to Monica the very thing she'd secretly feared for years. Hollis was Monica's mentor; he'd been assigned to her by an organization that pairs experts with small-business owners. A few years prior, when she launched her start-up aimed at teaching financial literacy to young women and girls, she filled out an online form requesting guidance about entrepreneurship—and Hollis was her match.

Fortunately, by the time he delivered this opinion, she knew to filter it out. But it had taken a lot of deep work to get there. Before she left her steady nine-to-five, she had started crafting her next act, distilling her ideas into a business that prioritized connection, community, and justice.

Then, she did the practical work of starting that business and making it profitable. Along the way, she did the introspective, even spiritual, work of recognizing her worth, despite the many internal and external forces that could have prevented her—including that old conditioning that equates relentless productivity with success, the constant demands of running a successful venture, and a world that values profit above all else.

A lot of personal work taught Monica that the primary job of any entrepreneur is knowing exactly what you stand for and ruthlessly shedding everything else. Although she appreciated the help Hollis had given her in the past, his latest advice wasn't for her.

Sure, she could have accepted this limiting belief. Our world continually shoves Hollis's message in our faces: Business is callous. You can help others or help yourself, so what's it going to be?

Monica refused then, and still refuses now, to play by the old-school rules of success. She sees her business as a tool to uplift humanity and ensure it isn't treated as an afterthought. It's her most immediate opportunity to find personal fulfillment and empower her community, while owning all forms of her wealth—time, talent, wellness, and yes, money. Though for decades she was convinced that prosperity wasn't for her—she is an educator and a do-gooder, after all—she's too fierce to let those stories keep her small. Like you, like me, she is a big-hearted entrepreneur.

## Doing the Deep Work

I relish running Teach Your Thing, my consultancy that helps purpose-driven businesses create education experiences that improve lives. As a learning design strategist and recovering employee (primarily at the Minnesota History Center, a major museum that was, in many ways, a life-giving place to work—until, for me, it wasn't), I love that this venture I built from the ground up has become a means for feeding the change I want to see in the world and in myself. I love calling the shots about how, when, and where I do my work. Exploring new ways to live out my highest contribution never gets old. And thanks to entrepreneurship, I've built a life that puts me in contact with changemakers who create positive ripple effects everywhere they go. I call these loving disruptors "big-hearted entrepreneurs." They are my mentors, peers, and clients, and many have become dear friends. They are givers who share their knowledge almost compulsively. They are kindhearted souls who can't unsee the pain in the world. And yet, they're not pushovers; they are doers who make things happen. They are optimists and creatives with enough vision to solve real problems—and the guts to make it happen. Through their businesses, they do things like train community agencies on trauma interventions, teach nonprofits how to raise money, and facilitate workshops on diversity, equity, and inclusion (DEI).

I help loving disruptors develop the workshops, courses, and signature talks that empower their people, increase their impact, and build income streams. Together, we take their big, sprawling idea and boil it down into something manageable. We identify what parts lead to the biggest lightbulb moments and organize their content into steps. We do practical things like write learning objectives and select the right platform for their lessons. But learning design is magical too. It guides us to tell stories and galvanize people into action.

As my clients discover, effective teaching isn't about content: it's about bringing people together, then crafting the right container to guide their transformation. Regardless of what they come to me for, we always dig into their deeper motivations.

This is where the fun comes in.

This is where we encounter their big-hearted best. This is where we suss out their unique value and help them own what truly sparks their fire. And this is where we decide how teaching and learning can amplify the mission they bring to the world.

## What Lights Your Fire?

Could you also benefit from harnessing what makes you and your business unique? Are you ready to give your content a home so more people can access your message? Is your impact dampened by everyday demands or traditional norms? I wrote this book to encourage more changemakers like you to own your worth, personally and professionally, so you can amplify a mission that matters to you. I base these lessons on my own experimentation, reflection, and learning as a business owner, as well as on methodologies I've practiced for decades as a professional educator. This book is for you if:

- You're a current or aspiring entrepreneur who's deeply driven to change your community for the better.
- You don't buy into the common narrative that business is only about the bottom line.
- You're a trailblazer who's tired of staying small when it comes to your time, energy, talent, and money.
- You yearn to bring an empowering message to the world through writing, speaking, or teaching, but struggle to prioritize it.
- You love to share your knowledge but get overwhelmed by too many ideas.
- You're ready to bring more humanity to an economy that extracts from individuals, communities, and our planet.

While writing this book, I reached out to a collection of changemakers and asked if they'd share their experiences of big-hearted entrepreneurship with me. I hope you're inspired by their stories of resilience, joy, and growth, which you'll find as quotes throughout the book.

Let's kick things off with Austin-based author Bethany Hegedus. She runs two businesses—The Writing Barn and Courage to Create—through which she nurtures a community of writers. During our interview, she captured the vision I want to be a reality for more of us big-hearted entrepreneurs:

*Gone are the days when we needed to be ashamed about money. The more we make, the more we can further our mission. Business can't just be about the bottom line; it has to be about the mission. The idea that you must either be mission-oriented or bottom line–oriented is part of why our systems are broken.*

*Maybe you've burned out pursuing your mission and don't have it in you to take care of yourself or take breaks when you need to. Or maybe you've ignored your soul for money, afraid that caring too much makes you weak. It's time to watch the results of your efforts, and the people around you, grow. It's empowering when the revenue starts to increase because it means you can increase staff wages.*

*I never thought this would be possible for me. I'm able to take care of the people around me in a new way—not just myself or my family, but also the people who work for me and who are part of my wider community.*

I'd love nothing more than for you to build your own version of the life Hegedus describes.

In this book, we won't do this by talking about business models; instead, we'll cover taking ownership of your worth as a big-hearted entrepreneur so that you can use your voice to amplify a mission that matters to you and your people. This means going deep. Cultural messages tell us what we can and can't do, and many of these messages are entrenched around us and within us. Growing into the full expression of the leader you are called to become isn't easy, but if you're anything like me, it's a quest that won't let you go.

Being a big-hearted entrepreneur is about becoming fully expressed as the **loving disruptor you are called to become.**

## Ditch the Old Rules of Success

For the fifteen years I worked at the Minnesota History Center, I believed money was awkward to talk about and that wealth meant greed. I thought educators like me had to sacrifice our time, talent, and money to make a difference. Now, I'm convinced that ideas like this are damaging to anyone, and that they can crush an entrepreneur. In our capitalist society, accepting these limits means we inherently diminish our own power—and our capacity to do good and uplift others along with it.

To thrive in today's economy, we must let go of these old rules of success. Below is a list of some of the biggies that held me back for years. What about you? If they're no longer serving you, pay attention. Paired with them are new rules you can use to guide your way and of course, you've probably already written a few of your own.

| OLD RULES OF SUCCESS | NEW RULES OF SUCCESS |
| --- | --- |
| Work should feel hard. | Sustainable work requires taking care of yourself. |
| Fit in. | Be uniquely you. |
| Ask permission for opportunity. | Seek your own opportunity. |
| Mass markets rule the day. | Today's marketplace supports infinite niches. |
| Business extracts from people and our planet. | Business is a tool for nurturing humanity and resources. |

| | |
|---|---|
| Professionals must choose mission or money. | We are reimagining our economy to rise above this disempowering belief. |
| Success is linear. | Success builds on a body of work, winding along the way. |
| Soft skills are fluff. | Self-awareness, empathy, and listening are critical business strategies. |
| Business is for cocky mavericks. | Business is for resilient community builders. |

As you work through the exercises in this book, you're likely to bump up against some tired expectations. But as a leader, you know better than to let them quiet your voice. As you continue to craft your own rules, I trust they'll unearth possibilities for you, your business, your clients, and the wider community you serve.

## How to Use This Book

In part one, "Own Your Worth," you'll explore how to invest your time, energy, and talent with love. And in part two, "Amplify a Mission That Matters," you'll encounter strategies and tactics to arrange your ideas, find the right container for them, and cultivate the warm connections needed to propel the change you yearn to see.

Each chapter ends with reflection prompts. Designed for journaling, they're meant to help you define your strategy, shape your story, navigate the marketplace, and get to know the future of work—in our changing world and for you personally. If you don't already have a journal, go get one. It can be as humble or as fancy as you like.

As far as I'm concerned, making things pretty is part of the fun, so every chapter also includes an exercise for creative expression. My own art journal is filled with watercolors and washi tape. I use it whenever inspiration strikes, or to get out of my head and into my hands. (Overthinkers, who's with me?) Gather some colorful supplies of your own and remember that this isn't about creating a masterpiece, it's about putting your ideas on paper.

Finally, each chapter ends with a quick task you can do to bring the content to life. Let's get started!

PART ONE

# OWN YOUR WORTH

**PART ONE** is about owning your worth in all its forms. Staying healthy as a mission-driven entrepreneur takes deep internal work, and I invite you to visit and revisit these chapters in any order as you grow yourself and your business.

# Get to Know Your Personal Medicine

"You have medicine that you must own." This quote comes from Jeffrey Davis, the founder of a consultancy and learning community called Tracking Wonder. I consider him a mentor, and his rallying cry has motivated my work since he said it in a webinar the year before I started my business. Since then, I've watched him live out this message consistently; his success as an author and podcaster never pulls him away from his mission of helping leaders make meaning in our productivity-focused world.

For me, his words hint at the beauty of what big-hearted entrepreneurship can be by making two key assumptions: one, that we are all singularly capable of healing others, and two, that some of us are pushing our best qualities away. The quote also captures one of my favorite parts of my work as a strategist for education experiences: helping changemakers own their exceptional purpose. That's my unique mission.

You might think purpose-driven founders like us could easily claim our highest contribution. After all, didn't we go into business, at least in part, because of a problem we yearn to solve? The answer is almost certainly yes! But even though big-hearted entrepreneurship requires us to embody our true genius, many things get in the way.

We're often too close to our work to see the differentiators that are evident to others. Even for those who've established a thriving client base, nurturing our medicine is critical for maximizing it. As circumstances evolve and we ourselves grow, so too does our capacity to do good.

Big-hearted business owners are notorious for generating new opportunities. This is an advantage in many ways, but we also tend to be people pleasers—high achievers who say yes to everything and everyone. Skillful at reading what's expected of us, we do that, then figure out how to exceed expectations. Is this process impressive? Often, yes. But is it profitable or even sustainable? Um, no.

Another double-edged sword is the ability to constantly come up with new ideas. Does this sound familiar? If you are used to seeing gaps and filling them all, then you likely know how easy it can be to lose sight of the contribution you're called to bring forth. But if you want to generate momentum, tap into the vibration of what makes you, *you*. Seek the courage to narrow your focus to what you do best. Then, put up blinders to anything that pulls you away from it.

I'm no stranger to the challenge of identifying your unique mission and trusting it. As I discovered over time, accessing this power depends on four factors working together:

- The **people** you're suited to serve
- A **problem** that breaks your heart
- The **tasks** that energize you
- The **outcomes** people will pay you for

This chapter explores people and problems, while chapter 2 looks at tasks and money.

## People You're Uniquely Suited to Serve

Your solution comes from a unique combination of knowledge and heart, and your business is a tool for spearheading progress. But until your people act—by buying (and using) your product or service—your special sauce can't help them. That said, you can't fix everything. You'll need to design your offerings for your treasured people, the ones you most want to elevate. Sure, we live in a hyper-connected world that lets us find people anywhere, any time. But today's economy is one of infinite niches, not mass markets. Focus on those who light up when they hear about your way of looking at the world. My clients are never clueless about who their people are, but the pull to reach more audiences is strong. Before they can own their true value and do their best work, they sometimes need to narrow their focus by serving a smaller segment of a broader audience. When considering who you're uniquely suited to serve, focus on right here, right now. Don't get lulled into thinking that what worked five years ago still works best today. I hung on to two audiences for years, determined to serve them both. When I finally named the focus that's right for me, I released a burden by letting one of those audiences go. Immediately, new clarity emerged. I stopped wasting time on a program with inconsistent results and before long, I replaced it with an improved version for the right people. A client of mine found an equally effective solution by developing two versions of his program, each speaking directly to a different audience segment.

Think about your treasured people. What common thread makes you care about them so much? Why would they come to you for help? Get clear on what unites them. Is it demographics, such as gender, age, or job title, or is it their motivations? Speaking to your peoples' attitudes and aspirations influences your ability to serve them authentically. Being unapologetic about who you are takes courage, but it's also what attracts the people who need you the most.

## A Problem That Breaks Your Heart

"What breaks your heart is part of your destiny." So says another favorite mentor of mine, who also happens to be Oprah's favorite guest of all time. Her name is Dr. Tererai Trent, and she's a Zimbabwean American author and a global advocate for universal education. When I attended her 2018 workshop in Santa Fe for a small group of women leaders, I instantly knew that I was in the presence of one of the most dynamic humans I'd ever encountered.

Though I didn't yet have her words to describe my journey, I was already on a quest to solve a problem that breaks *my* heart: Too many purpose-driven professionals yearn to make an impact in the world, but their deep gifts remain untapped. They have solutions for making their communities better, yet their highest contributions get held back year after year.

My client Liz Dempsey Lee—a Boston-area DEI educator for school districts, parent and community groups, and corporations—articulates this problem well: "I spent

To claim your true genius, you must give yourself permission **to let go of what no longer serves you.**

a lot of my life feeling like I had all these ideas and wasn't able to implement them. If I had been able to overcome that block earlier, I would have been on this path longer. And I'm pretty happy where I am."

Frustrated by the lack of dialogue about DEI in white communities, she decided to address the problem that breaks her heart by leading these conversations herself. Dempsey Lee is more than qualified to discuss education policy: she's a PhD, an adjunct professor, a school committee member, and a lifelong educator with experience teaching pre-kindergarten through to grade 8. As a parent who enjoys being around people, she's uniquely suited to creating a safe, relevant space for hard conversations. "I seem to be able to talk to anybody," she says. "I especially enjoy having conversations with people who have radically different belief systems than my own."

The topic of privilege is central to her programs. "It's important to bring people who are white like me, and what Robin DiAngelo [author of *White Fragility*] calls 'white adjacent,' meaning having some sort of proximity to whiteness—like my husband, who's Chinese American—into the lived experiences of other people." And as she points out, "just because some don't like the word 'privilege' doesn't mean it's not true."

As a big-hearted entrepreneur yourself, you may hesitate to amplify your true mission because you're buried under the weight of work that dances near what you really want to say. Rather than focusing on your true power, you operate nearby. You sense the pain of deep work undone, but you're too busy with current responsibilities to think straight about making changes.

Maybe you're haunted by the specter of what's expected of you, what feels familiar, or what once drove you but has since evolved. As a dreamer who believes you can solve big problems, you may have a hard time admitting you can't fix everything. You may take on new responsibilities while clinging for dear life to the old ones. But to claim your true genius, give yourself permission to let go of something. Ask yourself: What am I spending time on that drains me? What could someone else do better? Identify what no longer sparks your fire, then find a way to stop doing it.

Another one of my clients knew deep down that her personal mission had shifted. And yet, for over a decade, she'd built such a successful business that adapting it was daunting.

Anne Ingersoll of College Bound Associates helps high school students navigate the college admissions process. As the first person in her family to attend college, she cares about increasing access to post-secondary education. But over time another problem emerged, and its urgency wouldn't let her go.

"When I first started my business, my motto was simplifying the college process," Ingersoll says. "And I would still say that is what I've done in the last ten or twelve years. But over the years, I've also seen an increase in teen anxiety. It takes many forms: anxiety about social media, academics, failure, and fulfilling or maybe not fulfilling their parents' expectations about where they should go to college." In addition to facing everyday challenges like sleep deprivation and overwhelm, students and parents are bombarded with the chatter of opinions about schools.

Ingersoll's passion as a mindful college consultant is helping families embrace the concept that choosing the right college isn't about prestige, it's about finding the best fit. As she points out, "society tells us we need to be busy. Being busy leads to more productivity, and more productivity leads to more money. In addition to that, [society tells you that your] success depends on the name of the college you attend, which I disagree with. I've seen it time and time again. My mission is to help students keep focused on what's best for them, not only for their future career but also for their fulfillment from a quality-of-life perspective. There are too many pressures put on high school students. Nobody's asking, 'Does it bring you joy?'"

A certified yoga instructor, Ingersoll incorporates mindfulness into her conversations with families. She even wrote a blog series about how to breathe (expansively into the ribs) through the college application process. Teen anxiety is rising and can cause serious problems like headaches, substance abuse, and even suicide. For those who are college-bound in a world that can feel increasingly threatening, today's culture of achievement is a dire problem. Ingersoll guides students and parents to stay grounded through applications, essay writing, and even the (often damaging) college-driven chat around the holiday table.

When we see businesses making shifts like the one Ingersoll's made, the move may seem like a slam dunk. But developing and implementing a new strategy takes incredible time and effort. Owning a new identity takes guts. Even well-established leaders face obstacles like the imposter syndrome that can accompany starting anything new, especially in industries that thrive on status and ego. But if you, like Ingersoll, have a mission that breaks your heart, it may not let you go until you find a way to honor it.

## ⑦ REFLECT

- "You have medicine that you must own." What's one thing you could do to live out this quote this week?
- How might you own your personal medicine this year?
- What problem in your life or work breaks your heart and relates to your business mission?
- What solution have you found to this problem?
- Identify a category of people who face this problem too.
- Why are you uniquely suited to serve them?
- Do you find yourself stuck on a problem that's near your true mission, yet leaves you feeling unfulfilled?

## ☆ MAKE IT PRETTY

Draw your own version of the Venn diagram on page 17. Use light watercolors for each circle—that way, when your ideas intersect, the overlapping colors will look good. Pay attention to these intersections because they reveal something about your highest contribution. Inside or around each section of the diagram, jot down notes about what makes your business stand out and why.

## ♡ BRING IT TO LIFE

Powerful insights emerge when you name actual people, not just avatars, who represent your audience. Name three real people in your life who embody your ideal audience. Thinking about them one at a time, take notes on the following:

- What does this person aspire to?
- What do they have in common with the others?
- What problem can you help them solve?
- What holds them back from taking action?
- What happens after they come to you?

# Be Profitable and Sustainable

As a recovering employee and a woman, I know what it's like to be rewarded for doing too many things. By piling on more and more, you bury your juiciest talents. Sometimes they settle so deep that you forget what they look like. When I realized my initial business structure was profitable but not sustainable, I had to dig deep. To envision my business well into the future, I needed to ruthlessly prioritize my tasks by highlighting the ones that brought me energy and dramatically de-emphasizing the others.

Of course, running any business requires doing things you don't like. (Raise your hand if you're a creative visionary whose soul goes dark at the thought of file organization. Good God, I'm shivering right now!) But that doesn't mean you personally have to take them all on. Most business owners will tell you to get help with tasks you don't enjoy as soon as you can, and I agree wholeheartedly! Even so, knowing you should do something and actually doing it aren't the same thing.

For social enterprises, doing too much can feel inevitable. After all, it's no cakewalk to solve business problems while addressing a bigger community issue. Yet, thriving in today's creator economy means maximizing your gifts. Psychologist and bestselling author Gay Hendricks uses the term "genius zone" to describe the state in which human beings make big leaps in life and do the work that leads to their highest contribution. He compares it to the trap of our "excellence zone," where we're wanted and needed but rarely feel fulfilled.

You cannot afford to put finding fulfillment on the back burner. Defining your purpose shouldn't be an afterthought; it can lead to business growth and even stability. Today's marketplace requires all entrepreneurs, particularly bighearted ones, to discover and own what makes them special.

## Stop Undervaluing Your Gifts

As you zero in on your unique mission, consider both hard and soft skills. It's time to let go of the outdated idea that soft skills are frivolous. In our economy of infinite niches, soft skills have just as much, if not more, value than the hard ones. Sure, hard skills matter—they're teachable qualifications that deliver outcomes. But if you're undervaluing your innate skills, you're holding back an essential part of your medicine. Whatever you do, find a way to highlight the innate talents that make you and your team members unique. These qualities can include the following:

- Staying calm in chaos
- Lighting up a room
- Having artistic flair
- Envisioning the future
- Leading with emotional intelligence
- Having a wicked sense of humor
- Loving order and structure
- Holding space for others

Talent is a key resource for your business, and you can't afford to waste it. In a world that values productivity over all else, owning our gifts is countercultural, but necessary.

When Algernon Hall built his business, Jubilee Children's Entertainment, he learned not to suppress his God-given talent. His full-throttle energy inspired me when we met in an online course for entrepreneurs, and I've been following his work ever since. Hall describes the power of owning his creativity, a skill he brings to the Philadelphia-area school programs he delivers with this team. When things get hard, his mission keeps him going:

*I have a heart for kids growing up in the inner city. There were a lot of things that I didn't get growing up in East Orange, New Jersey. Then, this purpose surfaced when I was in my graduate program. I started to do some deep soul-searching and realized that I was creative. I really started to think about what I enjoyed. Even when I finished the program, I didn't identify as an entrepreneur. There were a lot of different things I dabbled in for money. Not that I wasn't good at it—I wasn't passionate about it. There was no mission attached to it. And when you're doing things just for money, you're missing something. Now, when things get difficult, that love fire burns deep. I love this thing so much that it really doesn't matter.*

## Deliver an Outcome That Pays

Mission-driven business owners like us are notorious for getting lost in our big ideas, and we're also known for undervaluing ourselves and our services. As someone who spent decades subconsciously believing wealth meant greed, I still struggle with this. On some level, so does just about every mentor, peer, and client I interviewed for this book. If you too have been told that working from the heart means you shouldn't care about money, then you have unlearning to do as well. (In a capitalist society, this belief is inherently disempowering.)

Embracing your talent is a key part of big-hearted entrepreneurship. That said, people won't just flock to you simply because you're living your passion. If you're new to business or launching a new offering, you need to find proof that people will pay for it. You may get pulled into doing too much for too little, so pay attention.

Nailing down the scope of your solution can be challenging. You are a big thinker who sees big problems that break your heart, but you may struggle with specificity. To provide an outcome your customers want (and will buy), make sure your offering is packaged in a clear, focused way, and that they know how it will be delivered. Take time to get feedback from your treasured people as you develop it and

You cannot afford to put finding fulfillment **on the back burner.**

listen for the problems that you can uniquely solve. Over and over, you'll need to give yourself permission *not* to fix every issue they have.

Twin Cities–based conscious sales coach Jason Jones, CEC, PCC, founder of The Coaching Hour, puts it this way: "One of the big Achilles heels of passionate, mission-driven folks is that they're out to impact the world. What's missing is they don't get the context from the people they serve. Instead, they just go around talking about how they want the world to be a better place. Everyone agrees, but no one's gonna buy."

For more than a year, Jones and I worked together to formalize his training program, Adaptive Conversations for Conscious Sales. Through this interactive workshop series, he guides coaches and sales teams to reject the traditional notion that selling is pushy. In fact, mission-driven providers can sell more (and be more at ease) when they connect with customers on a human level. As Jones says, "learn how to open up and be vulnerable yourself so someone else can be open with you."

Jones's method involves asking questions about the problems your prospects are facing, then (shocking!) listening for the answers. "The objective is to get really clear on what's important to them, what needs to be solved, and whether you have a solution for that or not. People spend money to solve problems. If you're solving a real problem that makes a difference and has value in the world—that's clearly defined in really, really simple terms that resonate in the context of how people experience their life and work—you will sell way more," he explains.

Running a business costs more money than you think, and it costs valuable time and energy. Straight up: helping others doesn't mean playing small. If you're struggling with guilt or something else that holds you back from charging what you're worth, those costs will add up and your mission will languish.

## Focus on Your Worth

I can't say this enough: you don't have to solve all your clients' problems. Seriously, stop for a second and say it out loud. I was in business for several years before I grasped this. One day, I was struck with the transformative realization that my clients don't need, or even want, me to fix everything for them! (*Whaaaat?*) What they need from me is clarity. They want to know what I'll do and how I'll do it. That's all.

If you don't tell your clients otherwise, they may ask you to jump in when a random problem pops up. Is this because they're unreasonable? No. I've come to understand that uncertainty and scope creep go hand in hand. In today's niche marketplace, it's your job to tell people what it means to work with you.

Massachusetts-based DEI facilitator Angele Goss no longer wastes energy believing she must become the be-all-and-end-all resource for her clients. Initially, she worried about what she didn't know rather than focusing on what she does know. "Because I work with different industries, I don't know all of them. There may be some regulation or timeline history that I don't know." But over time, Goss has embraced the high value she brings as a trained educator and DEI specialist. She has learned to overcome her old insecurities by bringing clarity to the experience, for herself and for the client. "There are a couple of ways I've had to really look at who I am and what I bring. I shift the focus from 'I'm the expert' to 'I'm here to facilitate this conversation.'"

Like many big-hearted entrepreneurs, Goss needed to remind herself that the thing she does beautifully is not something anyone can do. To the contrary, her innate brilliance contributes directly to the outcome her clients pay her for. Add to that her years of experience and training, and undercharging becomes even more damaging. Inadequate pricing not only threatens her health and sustainability but also kills her potential to make a difference.

"My mission is to help people facilitate conversations that are sometimes taboo in terms of race relations or differences, and then to help broaden their sense of community in their environment," says Goss. Guidance through tough dialogue is worth paying for. No longer concerning herself with unneeded tasks, Goss has increased her value proposition. She finds herself feeling more present, and her overall stress has gone down.

One of my favorite business books, *We Should All Be Millionaires: A Woman's Guide to Earning More, Building Wealth, and Gaining Economic Power*, teaches women and other marginalized folks to stop denying their worth. Author Rachel Rodgers tells it straight: "Instead of worrying about offending other people with your pricing, start worrying about your own broke-ass pockets. Worry about the fact that you don't have adequate health care or funds to retire. Worry about the stress you are under trying to make ends meet. Worry about the legacy you want to leave behind. In other words, worry about things you can actually control, and let go of other people's opinions."

When we try too hard to prove ourselves as purpose-driven leaders, we dilute our most precious assets: money, time, and energy. If we intend to address the deep problems in our world, wasting resources isn't just a missed opportunity—it's a travesty that blocks us from realizing our mission. It also keeps us from pursuing leadership, transformation, and growth.

> ## ⓘ REFLECT
>
> - Describe how one of your innate gifts provides a valuable outcome for your clients.
> - Are there job-related tasks that once gave you energy but now wear you out? Be brutally honest with yourself.
> - How does undervaluing your gifts prevent you from realizing your mission?
> - What do you want to be known for?
> - Are you solving a problem that you don't need to solve for clients? What is it?
> - What emotions come up as you consider narrowing your offering?

## ☆ MAKE IT PRETTY

Fill an entire page with a wash of watercolor. Put a big heading at the top, such as "Investing My Precious Energy." Write and draw images on the painted page in response to this question: If you could free up more energy by not doing the draining things, what would you put that energy toward instead? (Think like an investor. Whatever you put energy into should generate at least 10 percent growth over time, if not considerably more.)

## ♡ BRING IT TO LIFE

The next time someone asks what you do, tell them about your unique mission. Don't just give them your title or your business's name. Tell them about the problem that breaks your heart and who you uniquely serve. Keep it short but share why it matters to you. Notice how they respond, as well as how you feel when you say it.

# 3

# Power Up

"You're not corporate enough." These words were spoken to me in a hushed tone, the kind that tells you the speaker is trying to shield you from something or keep your dignity intact.

I was hurt of course, but it wasn't the time for that. The shame spiral would come; I would later play the statement over and over in my mind in a feeble attempt to rewrite this lunch. But for now, that wasn't my focus. It couldn't be. After all, I had a farmer's omelet to eat, and perhaps more importantly, a job to save.

I'd just completed my first assignment as a free agent after two decades of full-time employment. I was invited to lunch by a project coordinator at the instructional design agency that had contracted me to develop a corporate training course. For the past three months, I'd worked full time writing modules for their sales team.

I handed in the final lesson the week before, and the project coordinator requested we go out to lunch. I knew something was up, and before long, I found out what. For good or bad, she didn't mince words. "You're a skilled writer, but we feel you're not corporate enough for this client."

Was there ever a moment when you wished time would slow down, just for a second, so you could figure out what was going on? I had no idea what she was talking about. I did a quick mental scan, trying to pull up something, anything, that would explain her statement.

I thought about the one-on-ones I'd conducted with the client's representative to develop frameworks for the training. I thought we'd hit it off while brainstorming ways to onboard the sales staff to the company's protocols. I scoured my brain for some incident during the team meetings, where I'd gathered ideas from stakeholders in a state-of-the-art conference room. I flashed back to the hours I'd spent in front of my home computer, routinely giving up things like proper lunch breaks and weekend jaunts with my neighbors. My mind came up blank; nope, I couldn't come up with a single example of client disagreement.

What in the world justified my newfound label? This feedback was a first in my career. If you'd asked me ahead of time what we'd be discussing today, my unsuitability for an entire business sector would not have made the list. Though I consider myself the self-aware type, I was stunned that her proclamation held no meaning for me whatsoever.

So I asked, "Can you give me an example of what you mean?" Evidently, one of the metaphors I wrote in a training module, that of planting and growing seeds, didn't sit right with the company. When I told her the idea had been provided by the client rep himself, she said that didn't matter, that I should have known what to filter out.

But that wasn't all. "We're concerned about your overuse of the word 'authentic.'" She explained the team was worried what might happen if their sales training mentioned that word too many times. After some follow-up discussion, our lunch ended on friendly terms. The agency never hired me again.

Looking back now, it's clear that experience gave me a gift, though I couldn't see it at the time. For the next few days, I sporadically muttered to myself, "Corporate? *I can be corporate!*" Before long, I started to embrace a deeper realization: companies aren't the only ones who get to choose whether they work with an employee or contractor; the reverse is true as well. This idea was new to me. While I'd always worked for organizations I truly believed in, I'd grown up in a world where finding opportunity meant asking for permission. Employers had the upper hand, and it rarely occurred to me or my colleagues to prioritize our own needs and talents.

Now, my plea to you is to reject the notion of rejection. As a business owner, you're sure to receive your share of nos. When you do, ask yourself whether the relationship was misaligned in the first place. If you are being asked to put your values on hold, or even hold them back, you are not standing in your power. You are not serving your true mission.

## Speak Your Message Your Way

Authenticity isn't a bad word. Genuine connection, trustworthy dialogue, and even empathetic sales practices are values worth standing for when running your own show.

**Reject the notion of rejection.** As a business owner, you're sure to receive your share of nos.

Consider the example of Barb Buckner Suárez, founder of Portland-based company BBSuárez. Through workshops and classes, she guides people through the process of becoming parents. "On a deep, deep level, what I'm most interested in is actually ending multigenerational trauma," she says.

To further this mission, Buckner Suárez resists traditional norms. "I think the cultural message of how to be a parent is bullshit. We've got a lot of people out there screaming, 'this is the way you should be parenting your kid! This is the book you should read!' I am not that person. I don't even like the idea of being a parenting expert."

Through classes, one-on-one coaching, and her podcast *Birth Happens*, Buckner Suárez is forthright in her approach. "The people who want to work with me want something different. I can kind of tell when somebody says to me, 'Hey, Barb, what's the best book I should get for my baby?' I say, 'your baby is your book,' and if they respond, 'you've got to be kidding me,' I figure we're probably not going to work together."

But when the right ones come along, they're ready to sign up. Her largest offering is a four-week series that takes eight to ten hours to complete, a commitment of both time and money for her audience. Because Buckner Suárez isn't shy about her style, parents who want an unconventional approach don't have to waste time researching options. "I'm gonna guess 95 percent of those people come as a warm, personal referral. In fact, I've had some people whose friends have bought them my class for new expectant parents. They're like, 'This is the one you want to take,' which is lovely and fantastic."

## Embrace the Power of Running Your Own Show

One of my proudest moments as a business owner came around three years into Teach Your Thing, when I picked up a client so completely aligned with my values that meeting him felt like a gift: Jason Jones of The Coaching Hour. He hired me to shape his program into a training series for sales teams and coaches. Empathy, listening, and trust were infused into every aspect of his business, and I was thrilled to support the endeavor. After a few months of working together, he became my first retainer client. As we inked the deal on this extended contract, it wasn't lost on me how far I had come.

A few years before, I'd been canned for bringing authenticity into sales training. Now, as a freelancer, I'd booked my biggest job yet... for doing that exact thing. Jones's conscious sales training doesn't just tout authenticity—it places it at its foundation.

For the next year and a half, Jones and I enjoyed collaborating on a variety of materials for his programs, from whitepapers to an operation manual to his ten-deck training series. Neither of us had to waste time explaining why our philosophies mattered; our shared commitment to humanity in business was an asset from the start. Never underestimate the magic of aligned values!

The arrangement proved profitable for us both—the programs we developed launched him into a successful new echelon, and the project brought me two new wonderful clients. Even now, I'm honored to have played a role in developing Jones's body of work, which disrupts the status quo of traditional push sales and ensures empathy is front and center.

When it comes to shaping your unique mission, you must trust that you're not the only one who believes in your values. Your people are out there. If you're spending your energy on projects that dilute what matters to you, you'll have a harder time gaining momentum. (Also, be prepared to spend more time in the pain of unfulfillment.) Projects may come along that pull you away from your values, so do what you can to resist them.

Had I continued working for agencies that never felt quite right, I wouldn't have met Jones or the other change-makers I highlight in this book. Standing strong in what you believe in can be risky, but as entrepreneurs know, calculated risks can pay off. Your return on investment may come in the form of time, energy, money, or—as in the case of my work with The Coaching Hour—all three.

## ⓘ REFLECT

- What does the word "power" mean to you: power over people, or the power to do something?
- Have you ever experienced a rejection that led to an opportunity?
- Do you have a personality quirk, nerdy interest, or countercultural value that someone (possibly yourself) has given you a hard time about?
- How can this quirk be viewed as a positive? What can you do to own it and leverage its power?
- How can taking a stand for something you believe in add to your power?

## ☆ MAKE IT PRETTY

Illustrate part or all of this quote in your journal. It comes from Christine Kane's transformative book *The Soul-Sourced Entrepreneur*: "*Power* is a weird word... It makes us think of evil regimes. Or hateful political agendas. If the idea of accessing or experiencing power makes you feel weary, this might be why... So, let me be clear about what I mean by power. For the soul-sourced entrepreneur, power is simply the energy to create things, to transform things, to evolve, to be clear. It's the ability to manage and direct your energies toward an outcome or end. That's all... It's 'power *to*.' Not 'power *over*.'"

## ♡ BRING IT TO LIFE

Make a list of content creators who use an authentic voice that resonates with you. They could be podcasters, authors, or influencers. Take ten minutes to enjoy their content. Consider how their style can inspire you to own your unique power.

# Leap!
## (A.K.A. Look for Lily Pads)

A FEW YEARS into entrepreneurship, an image popped into my head as I was trying to make a tough decision: a frog on a pond. Ever since, the metaphor of lily pad–jumping has helped me navigate business decisions.

Allow me to explain. Entrepreneurship has no single path to greatness. In a society that misunderstands big-hearted business, you need to act, again and again, without referencing many clear examples of success and without the ability to predict what will happen next.

Enter lily pads.

Unlike when you climb a traditional corporate ladder, which provides structure and direction, entrepreneurship requires you to hop around. Sometimes, you leap forward; other times, your moves may look lateral or even backward to an outside observer. But every lily pad provides a new viewpoint, revealing information and opportunities that weren't visible before.

Everything substantive I have achieved as a business owner—creating a cohort program, collaborating with my business heroes, and experimenting with a location-independent lifestyle—happened because I found the courage to leap from a familiar spot.

Building a business that allows me to spend a month each year in Albuquerque, New Mexico, as opposed to my residence near St. Paul, Minnesota, means family gatherings don't have to happen entirely over Zoom. (A nineteen-hour drive separates us, so time with them is precious.) This new habit has contributed to my well-being and overall sense of agency, opportunities every worker deserves.

## WHERE YOU WANT TO GO

## Some Outcomes Are Intangible, and That's Okay

Not all outcomes can be predicted—and some are intangible, especially to other people. Any time you leap, be ready for something to surprise and delight you.

For example, take writing this book. Would you consider this a forward leap? Ask my close friend Jennifer and she'll tell you my book is an undeniable vault forward. To her, creative expression and personal growth are commodities to be treasured; their transformative power should be prioritized as much as tangible results like possible new income streams. She cheered me on at every step, and I credit her for inspiring me to start writing in the first place. But ask an accountant and they may tell you it's a step backward. When viewed from the perspective of a profit-and-loss statement, the project may be tough to justify. After all, publishing a book requires considerable time, energy, and money.

What's a leap you're considering taking soon? If you're torn between competing priorities, get clear about what motivates you. Make sure your head and heart are in alignment. That may sound obvious, but if you find yourself caught in analysis paralysis, sussing out what your body needs (as well as your mind) may take time. I spent two months frozen in indecision about whether to move forward with publishing the book. Eventually, I admitted to myself that the benefits I sought didn't have to make sense to everyone. The outcomes of your leap may be hidden, especially to those whose opinions might be holding you back right now.

Case in point: During my revisions, I was shocked to encounter an unexpected payoff—the book helped me turn my entrepreneurial journey from a "me" into a "we." When I reached out to my community for quotes about their experiences as big-hearted entrepreneurs, their enthusiasm overwhelmed me and brought me to (gratified) tears more than once. I requested interviews with clients, mentors, and peers, and I'm pretty sure not a single person turned me down. My conversations with them were uplifting—not only was I emboldened by their passion but their stories helped to clarify ideas I'd been honing for years, largely on my own. And in the end, their responses transformed my message.

Entrepreneurship is notoriously isolating, but the act of writing this book reminded me that the big-hearted are everywhere and have surrounded me all along. As one of my interviewees pointed out, "There are more of us than you think!"

## Get Comfy with Calculated Risk

As a business owner, only you can determine which leaps are worth taking and why. As I see it, a leap is any opportunity that brings you noticeably out of your current comfort zone. For me, this generally involves major progressions, the kind that may take months to achieve. These are calculated risks, and as one of my clients, Whitney Brimfield, explains, entrepreneurs need to grasp the art of them.

Brimfield is the founder of Spark Point Fundraising, a Washington, DC–based development firm with a commitment to equity and impact. She and her staff support nonprofits with grant writing and fundraising services. Before starting her company, she helped a previous employer establish a new income stream by building a consulting practice within the organization.

Today, that practice provides a significant percentage of the company's revenue. But Brimfield points out that "it took a really long time for them to build because they were risk averse. They didn't want to put too much time and effort into something they didn't think was going to work. But as they started to see how it could be marketed and how it was relevant to their members and other constituents, it became more and more valuable to them and the folks in their field."

As she's done numerous times for herself, Brimfield encourages mission-driven founders to look for opportunities that represent calculated risk, ones that rely on their strengths but allow them to stretch.

Calculating risk involves research. "There are lots of things you can do before you take any risks, like hosting conversations with trusted advisors, and potentially clients, about your ideas and saying, 'How does this sound to you?'"

As with every business decision, you must decide what characterizes a desirable leap for you. But as the lily pads metaphor reminds us, you must let go of the idea that your progress will be perfectly linear or structured.

## Own Your Reasons for Leaping

Whenever you decide to leap, I encourage you to own your reasons and trust that something may unfold in a magical way you can't predict. Even when you experience setbacks or realize after the fact that there may have been a more direct route (that's called learning!), look for the lessons in the leap.

Consider again me writing this book. You may say my approach was backward. Looking back, even I think it sounds odd: I wrote a sixty thousand–word manuscript before it occurred to me to figure out how I'd publish it. No, I didn't research publishing options until after I'd captured my ideas on paper. Is this an approach I'd recommend to all aspiring authors for proven results? Well, no. Not exactly.

But I knew my reasons. I had an overwhelmingly strong instinct that this was the right move at precisely that time in my life and work. I'd been writing and editing for more than twenty years, both as an employee and a contractor. I'd been lamenting our inequitable economy, and I was tired of holding back a message I sensed could embolden others. And my business was ripe for a shift from a done-for-you model to one that could meaningfully scale. Also, I simply *wanted* to do it. For many of us, this may be the hardest thing to say out loud—but what's wrong with letting ourselves live a lifelong dream?

Though I'm absurdly grateful to have found the right publisher, having my words presented in this exact form wasn't something I was tied to when I wrote the first draft. But I trusted that my content was valuable. On some deep level that was hard to explain logically, I knew I would find a way to package it. After writing the draft, possibilities emerged that weren't visible when I started. When I dug into the revisions, I began to see how I could turn the chapters into in-person and online workshops. The vision became clearer with each round of edits.

This journey may not have the makings of a masterclass, but the risk I took was, in fact, a calculated one. It's also a reminder that leaps tend to reveal their sweetness only after we jump. What enchanted outcomes may emerge after you take your next leap? You can't possibly know now but consider the lily pads as you move toward growth.

## Growth as a Series of Lily Pads

Lily pads bring you closer to your goal on the other side of the pond, but they're rarely predictable. As you determine which leaps are right for you, consider these assumptions:

- You're working toward a goal; point A is on one side of the pond and point B is on the other.
- There are multiple possible paths for getting there.
- Your overall movement should honor the destination but expect some lateral or even "backward" moves.
- You get to decide what's progress and what's not.
- Over time, your own best path will reveal itself.
- Skipping lily pads isn't realistic.

That last point is so important. In his book *Company of One: Why Staying Small Is the Next Big Thing for Business*, Paul Jarvis argues that people tend to leave out key steps

When you experience setbacks or realize there may have been a more direct route, **look for the lessons in the leap.**

when telling business success stories. "Most of these speakers neglect to mention that they didn't just willy-nilly jump," he points out. "Rather, they did a small jump first to make sure they could land it."

Passion-driven entrepreneurs like us need to ensure there's demand for our offerings before devoting too many resources to developing them. Winning financial support is difficult for any venture, but it can be particularly challenging for socially conscious leaders. In addition to facing a crushing societal issue, they may also be seeking funding from organizations and community members who underestimate them, express cynicism, or misunderstand their goals. There's no way around it: addressing these obstacles takes time. Sustainability requires thoughtful, strategic growth. Leaps and emotions go hand in hand, especially for changemakers with big hearts. As you make bold moves, notice what comes up. Before moving to something new, do you need to grieve what's left behind? Even when we no longer want or need that thing, our emotions don't always get the memo. Society tells us otherwise, but honoring our feelings and processing them is courageous and wise, and it leads to better decisions. Does the growth you face trigger fear of some kind? Notice it in your body and acknowledge that too.

As Jarvis points out, our progress isn't predetermined—it reveals itself along the way. "I didn't start out with a passion to be a web designer, a writer, or an online course creator. I didn't even have the courage to jump headfirst into those jobs. They happened slowly after I owned my related skills to the point where they were in demand."

Though Whitney Brimfield had a strong vision from the start, Spark Point also grew in layers, with services evolving over time. "From the beginning of the company, we were specific about what we do: grant writing and foundation fundraising. Starting from that baseline, we had a leg up because there aren't a lot of entities that do that specific work." But it never would have reached its eventual capacity had she not paid close attention to what worked at every step. Today, Spark Point serves clients with budgets from under $500,000 up to $100 million.

One tactic Brimfield used was documenting the procedures that clicked while asking clients for feedback, both good and bad. "The more you do something, the more you see where the flaws are," she says. "When you come to a process with some knowledge of how to do grant writing or foundation fundraising, and then you layer your experience with many different organizations on top of that, you can see what works across the board and what doesn't."

Maybe, like Brimfield, you're a seasoned entrepreneur who is scaling your operations. Or maybe you're new to starting a business. No matter what message you're receiving about why passion and profit can't go together, keep trusting yourself and listening to what your people need. Let the path to your contribution develop on your time frame, one lily pad at a time.

## ⓘ REFLECT

- Name a leap you're contemplating right now.
- How far outside your current comfort zone might it take you?
- What data can you gather to weigh the decision?
- What is your comfort level with risk?
- Would you describe the leap as a calculated risk? Why or why not?
- What direction do you think this leap will take you in?
- Is it possible you may need to grieve something to make this leap?

## ☆ MAKE IT PRETTY

In your journal, illustrate lily pads on a pond. Draw them big, taking up an entire spread.

In the bottom left corner, note where you are now. In the top right corner, note where you want to be. Write an action you may take to get there in each lily pad. Keep in mind that your path is unlikely to be linear. You can't foresee everything, so these actions (or your destination itself) may change as you make moves. But visualizing what's possible now increases your chances of making big things happen.

## ♡ BRING IT TO LIFE

Find a time and place where you can be quiet for ten minutes. Close your eyes and think about your next leap. Pay attention to how it feels in your body and consider what that information means to you.

# 5

# Trust Your Inner Knowing

HUMAN BEINGS have inherent worth, but I'm convinced that to make leaps as a big-hearted entrepreneur, you must explore your worthiness on a deep, soul level—both as an individual and as an entity.

One of my clients, Laina Latterner, describes her spiritual journey as an entrepreneur: "It's challenging to get validation externally. Through this process, I realized I needed to have internal validation." Latterner is building a Twin Cities–based health hub for women called The ViFi (as in Wi-Fi for everyone with a vagina).

Latterner explains, "Everyone comes to their business with all their life experience. For me, it's not just bringing sales experience, but also my experience as a mom. I'm bringing experience as a patient in health care, as a salesperson who has talked to doctors, and as someone who has been silenced in the corporate world and told to stay in my lane on multiple occasions. I was told that if I work harder, I will get ahead. And that was not the case."

As an entrepreneur, trusting your inner knowing is crucial. Your body sends you signals about which decisions aren't right for you, but paying attention to these signals can be challenging. For Latterner, the journey toward entrepreneurship required listening to—then advocating for—her wisdom at every stage. When the rigid culture at an international public relations firm confined her, she took a different job at a medical start-up. She loved the people and the variety, but more importantly, her devotion to health care took root. This led to an opportunity to serve community health centers that lit her fire for health care reform. But when constant travel kept her from her family, she moved to a different organization. Based out of Switzerland, its culture championed women's health and doubled down on Latterner's passion for feminism, patient rights, and health care education.

After she landed her dream role supporting a sales team working with cutting-edge preventative health care products, a new CEO arrived, and her division was cut. From the outside, it may have seemed that Latterner's career had hit a dead end.

Fortunately, her long-standing habit of trusting herself served her well in entrepreneurship. When she received severance, she took a calculated lily pad risk and started The ViFi.

## Seek Your "Stretch Zone"

Succeeding in business means getting comfortable with the unknown; on the other hand, we can't make change if we're defeated or overwhelmed. To stay energized, purpose-driven leaders need to balance growth and security. Living in your comfort zone isn't the point; growth requires stretching. That said, being in a state of panic helps no one—not your people, and certainly not you.

College consultant Anne Ingersoll shared a graphic with me that speaks to "the stretch zone": the ideal place for fostering purpose-driven work.

The right leaps stretch you enough to gain new insights and encounter opportunities, but not so much that they threaten the boundaries you've set for your time, energy, or money.

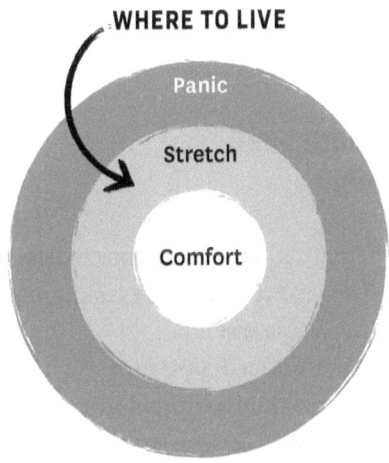

## Bring Your Body and Mind to the Decision

Understanding the distinction between positive growth and growth that infringes on our boundaries isn't easy. It requires consulting our logic without shutting down our intuition. According to *The Mind-Body Way: The Embodied Leader's Path to Resilience, Connection, and Purpose*, "the usual understanding of leadership is also filled with false dichotomies. When we make decisions with our heads and ignore our hearts ... we are forgetting that everything is connected. Embodied Leaders embrace the reality that the head and the heart, the mind and the body ... should be integrated for healthy leadership to happen."

Many of us in business, including me, struggle to overcome the deep conditioning that tells us the head is more valuable than the heart. When exploring your next leap, pay attention to your instincts. Do what you can to bring both your body and your mind to the decision.

## Don't Leap until Mind and Body Align

There's no inherent right or wrong time to leap to your next opportunity. The best timing is the timing that's right for *you*. Owning this fact is essential.

Personally, I've noticed a pattern: my inner knowing, the gut response that thinks without thinking, consistently proves to be the first to tell me I'm ready to take the next leap. In most cases, my head is nowhere near ready. Desperate to keep me safe, it produces a litany of logical reasons not to take the calculated risk.

Full disclosure: I'm not a big risk taker. For me, moving forward before my head is ready causes unnecessary anxiety. So, I've learned to wait—sometimes anywhere from three to nine months—until my head aligns with my gut.

This strategy has proved a comfort to me. Whenever I notice anxiety about a decision creeping in, rather than chastising myself, I stop and say, "Aha! I'm not a wimpy loser. I'm just in that phase: my instinct is ready for the next lily pad, but my head needs more time."

If I need to appease my logic, I gather data. Sometimes more information isn't necessary; I just need time to get used to a new idea. With most big decisions, my head eventually catches up, and I leap. Over time, I've also noticed that trusting my instincts has gotten easier. Indeed, the gap between the impulse to leap and the leap itself has shrunk.

Plus, looking back, it's clear that my instincts have always been right.

When it comes to your own leaps, start paying attention. Your instincts and your head will tell you when you're ready.

## Let Go of Shame

All too often, untrodden paths and shame go hand in hand. As a big-hearted entrepreneur, I've had to reject my desire to do what's expected and instead find the courage to live out what's best for me and my business.

I no longer work for someone else, but I'm still sometimes haunted by the specter of traditional expectations. Outdated norms can show up in conversations with strangers, acquaintances, and loved ones. If you are the caring type who wants to be liked, you may feel bombarded by fear of doing the wrong thing. Some of my wisest leaps have been to lily pads that, from a hierarchical worldview, looked like lateral or even backward moves.

Embracing a life of resilience requires letting go of the shame that accompanies traditional expectations. In her book *Body of Work: Finding the Thread That Ties Your Story Together*, Pamela Slim normalizes "continually inventing and relaunching" your brand. As you jump from one place to the next, Slim says:

> *You won't have to say things like, "I am throwing away ten years of studying and practicing law" if I start a yoga studio. (Don't worry—your relatives will say it.) Or "I am undermining my potential if I take a job as a barista" after you get laid off from your corporate job as a highly paid creative. If your body of work is about creating beauty and art, why not make lovely images in latte foam while you retool for a new job?*

Those of us who've internalized old-school rules of success can't hear Slim's message enough! Navigating these moves can be tricky. Sometimes a leap brings progress in one area while seemingly hindering you in another. A classic example of this is saying no to clients to give yourself space to develop a new program or offering. When making an unconventional move like this, you may be more vulnerable to fear, guilt, or doubt.

If you're anything like me, you may experience analysis paralysis when it comes to spending money. One category that tends to trigger unseemly emotions is professional development. Keeping up with industry trends and refreshing our skill sets increases our capacity to serve clients effectively and run smooth operations. But courses, masterminds, conferences, and coaching can be expensive, which can trigger shame.

To make leaps as a big-hearted entrepreneur, **you must explore your worthiness on a deep, soul level.**

We can't know ahead of time which programs will bring an exponential return on investment and which will become losses of time, money, or energy. When a stakeholder disagrees about what's worth it and what's not—say, your business partner, CPA, or spouse—decisions become even more fraught. One leader's investment is another's waste of resources. Old rules of success may crop up as well, making you question your choice to move forward. Here, you'll need to lean extra hard on your inner knowing. Even when you and "they" (a specific person or a societal norm) disagree, you'll be better prepared to find a solution if you can articulate why the program is important to you or the business.

When investing in yourself or your team, emotions are part of the deal. Know yourself so you can honor these emotions but not allow them to take over. As for me, I've learned to navigate this when making decisions about money. When my logic and my instincts don't agree at first, I wait until I'm ready. I need to get quiet and discern what's right for me.

## Stop and Look Around

Discernment is critical not only for strategy and sustainability but also meaningful connection. In short, it's key to becoming our best selves. To gain wisdom, we must stop, breathe, and take a good long look around.

Unfortunately, big-hearted entrepreneurs are known for living on the edge of burnout. Relational overachievers like us can't unsee problems, and we convince ourselves that working harder will finally make a dent in them.

I see the habit of relentless productivity in myself and my clients all the time. Achieving business goals while giving back to our communities asks a lot of us. We tend to give without question. But we can't make real change until we give ourselves space.

In his book *Permission to Glow: A Spiritual Guide to Epic Leadership*, Kristoffer Carter makes the case this way: "There's a paradox I see with the more seasoned leaders I coach. The demands on their time and attention continue to expand, and somehow, they keep optimizing toward light touch, high leverage, activities. This requires a commitment to living outside the weeds."

Are you living in the weeds of your business demands? Oh, my friend, I feel your pain. I know what unchecked busyness looks like. In my first phase as a business owner, I replicated the lifestyle I'd known as a mission-driven museum educator. Never taking vacations? Check. Feeling guilty if I took a break? Check. Believing I was the only one who could get things right? Yeah, duh! "Yes" was my favorite word, and I relished my ability to create high-quality work while squeezing every dime.

Though this chaos helped me feel needed—let's be honest, we with big hearts relish the feeling—it led to some of my worst decisions. As you navigate the lily pads of your own purpose-driven business, you must find a way to create margin. More importantly, you must trust that you're worthy of this space. I beg you to heed Carter's warning: "Space is allowed for increased demand. The greater the volatility, the more determined we must be to slow down and make better decisions."

## ⑦ REFLECT

- Is busyness getting in the way of your discernment? What can you do to give yourself more margin to think?
- Name a time when your inner knowing and your logic disagreed. What did you choose? What happened?
- Is a stakeholder questioning a decision you want to make? What does your inner knowing say?
- How can you process someone else's opinion in a way that honors the health of your business?

## ☆ MAKE IT PRETTY

Illustrate a decision you're trying to make. Draw a huge target diagram like the one on page 61, with three concentric circles labeled "Comfort Zone," "Stretch Zone," and "Panic Zone." Journal within the circles about what this means to you.

## ♡ BRING IT TO LIFE

Identify a decision you need to make. Block an hour on your calendar to focus on it, free of distractions.

# 6

# Do Your Deep Work

WHEN I think of founders who've seen their income and impact grow through owning their mission, I think of Bethany Hegedus, who runs a community for authors. She and I met in an online cohort program during my early days as a solopreneur, years before her second business was even an idea. In the years since, we've become dear friends, actively supporting each other's personal and professional growth.

I never tire of seeing the ways Hegedus meaningfully weaves together purpose and profit. She's a relentless champion for the values she holds dear, such as equity, creativity, and empowerment. Over time, I've watched her take increasing ownership of her worth as a leader and business owner. As Hegedus says, "The more I concentrate on my mission, the easier it is to make money—and the more empowered I feel when I raise my prices or when I see the long-term impact of working with someone."

Her programs also include one-on-one mentoring for authors. Through The Writing Barn, she also offers classes that range from ninety-minute webinars to six-month experiences. She's passionate about providing stability for teaching artists and writers, during an age when publishing is an almost impossible way solely to earn a living. At the time of our interview, she was launching the sixth cycle of her community, Courage to Create, which opens twice a year. "We're hoping for over four hundred members this time and we have 308 really active members right now, deeply rooted in the principles of a community garden," Hegedus says, referencing the values that drive her work. She's committed to transforming the country club model of traditional publishing to one of transparency and accessibility. She explains the dynamics of old-school publishing: "If you do get chosen, you think, 'That's a weird feeling. I'm in a club, but I don't know the rules. And I don't want to get kicked out. So, I'd better not ask any questions.' And before you know it, to fit in and stay in, you've disavowed your worth—and sometimes your true voice."

Instead, she brings a "garden philosophy" to every aspect of her community, from the speakers she hires to the audience interaction to the tone. "It takes many hands to grow the creative soil," she says. "We all get heard in our own time. We can all blossom when we pull our nutrients together and we give back as needed."

## Take Your Worth Seriously

Shona Ramchandani—founder of Chrysalis Consulting Collaborative, a justice, equity, diversity, and inclusion (JEDI) consultancy based in Minneapolis–St. Paul—started her business because she saw an urgent need for influential change in the world, starting with our workplaces. She launched her venture in 2020, smack-dab in the middle of a global pandemic and the same year that George Floyd's murder sparked a long-overdue retaliation against racist violence and police brutality. Many of our systems—including education, housing, and business—perpetuate structural discrimination, so the call for justice can't stop there. Ramchandani's career move required some serious gut checks: What would she take a stand for, and how would she go about it?

"A lot of times, I've let other people tell me my worth and my contributions," she says. But as Ramchandani embraced entrepreneurship, she began to shift the dynamic. "My business gave me the opportunity to name my values, and therefore the contributions I can make. As an employee, I didn't feel I had the capital—the social capital or power capital or title capital—to make the changes that were so desperately overdue. Ultimately, that led to starting my own business so I could try to offer something transformational."

At the time of our interview, she'd been running her consultancy for three years and was contemplating her next leap, prioritizing the values that drive her—particularly the need for sustainable systemic change.

"In my field, I find that what people think they know is different from reality. I genuinely believe people want to make change or they wouldn't invest money in hiring a consultant. When you invest in JEDI work, you are essentially investing in systems change. And I don't know how many organizations are ready to do that," she says.

## Search Your Soul

Ramchandani chooses her clients with intention; she seeks out those who are "willing to commit to a long-term journey" and ensure accountability at a systems level, ideally influencing other organizations in their field. She knows her ultimate destination: a business that catalyzes systemic change and provides her with the freedom, financial stability, and power capital to determine her next move forward. If the bottom line were all she cared about, perhaps her leaps wouldn't require as much soul-searching.

To get where she wants to go, Ramchandani could take her next leap in a variety of directions. There's no set path, only the one that's right for her. But the work she's done to take a stand for her values has improved her quality of life already. She enjoys a greater sense of agency than she did in her employee days, and she's generated the profit to empower the work of others she believes in.

For big-hearted entrepreneurs like Hegedus, Ramchandani, you, and me, making money matters, to be sure. But not if it comes at the cost of our values.

You can ditch traditional norms and make up your own, and you can do so in your own time and in your own way.

You can ditch traditional norms and make up your own. **Do it in your own time and in your own way.**

## ⑦ REFLECT

- What are your core values?
- How do you demonstrate your core values through your business operations?
- How are you taking your worth seriously right now? Where could you improve?
- How can soul-searching lead to empowerment, for you or within your offerings?

## ☆ MAKE IT PRETTY

Fill an entire page with a wash of watercolor paint. Put a big heading at the top: "Naming My Own Worth." Write about what this means to you on the painted page. Do the same thing on another page under the heading "Living My Core Values." Draw a relatively large circle on that same page. On the outside of the circle, write or draw ways you live your values outwardly—how you help family or volunteer in your community, for example. On the inside, show how you apply those values to yourself. Don't skip this last part. If one of your values is empowerment, list ways to honor your needs, boundaries, and right to have fun.

### ♡ BRING IT TO LIFE

Find one place, in person or online, where you can express a core value this week. Move beyond lurking and contribute to the conversation. Say something about an issue you care about, in your unique way, that reflects that value.

# Protect Your Energy

MEANINGFUL WORK is nonnegotiable, but mission doesn't justify unhealthy boundaries. For most of my professional life, I wanted to be a productivity superstar. I strove to solve all the problems, from daily tasks to social systems. Now, I know constant busyness is a liability. If left unchecked, perpetual productivity can lead to sloppy decisions and other damaging consequences. This is true for anyone, but for caring entrepreneurs who feel the weight of deep societal issues, the tolls of exhaustion are particularly devastating. According to Paul Jarvis in *Company of One*, "We make bad decisions when we are strapped for time, too busy to think, and struggling to manage our obligations. Even if we take only a few hours a week of unplanned time, we can develop a bigger-picture focus or strategies for how our business actually runs." I've learned to make space for time like this and it has become crucial for keeping my energy up. Never underestimate how tiring it can be to navigate constant decision-making. New entrepreneurs can struggle with calling the shots, while established ones can wrestle with the emotional toll of influencing their team members' livelihoods. Either way, it takes a lot out of you.

## Are Busy People Pushovers?

Being highly relational as a business owner is a valuable skill. Building relationships helps you attract clients, offer a personalized experience, and establish a strong reputation. But if you're not careful, a tendency toward interconnectedness can cost you.

If you tend to put others first, pay attention. Are you confusing kindness for people-pleasing?

In an article for The Journal, author Isaiah Hankel says that busy people are readily manipulated. He puts it this way: "When you are busy, it's easy for other people to make you feel like you only have one choice—theirs. Distraction turns people into pushovers. When grown men and grown women try to make you feel guilty for not spending time with them or not doing what they want, it's simply a power play."

Ouch! When I first read these words, I winced so hard you could practically hear it. One such interaction still irks me. On the edge of burnout in my second year of entrepreneurship, I became vulnerable to an aggressive sales pitch and wasted money on a service I didn't want—a high-end coaching package I'd been approached about several times. Exhausted and with too much on my plate, I lacked the filter to sort out my emotions, listen to my instincts, and say no. I agreed under pressure, despite my body's signals that it wasn't right. (After receiving the sales call, I emailed to cancel the arrangement but only got part of my money back.)

Now, my boundaries are clear. I know what I need and what matters to me. If someone's competing agenda comes along—and it always does—I recognize the potential risk to my priorities. Remember, you get to decide what matters to you, when, and why. Even if what you need may seem selfish, you have the right to stand up for it.

## When Mission and Resources Conflict

Entrepreneurship schooled me about opportunity cost. Sure, when I started my business, I already knew what the term meant: something you give up by choosing something else. But I'd been conditioned to do it all and ignore the effects on my energy. Triple-booked meetings were the norm for me as an employee, and juggling multiple projects felt like a badge of honor. I assumed being busy meant that I mattered, that my work was needed, and that I was a team player.

For years as a business owner, I replicated this habit. I'd be lying if I told you I've completely changed, but over time I've built a schedule that prioritizes space, strategy, and wellness. Overseeing my own venture has taught me that you can only ignore the consequences of overwork for so long. Sooner or later, the cost of what you're missing shows up. It appears in tangible ways, like on your profit and loss statement. If you spend hours and hours on a project that tugs at your heart but pays little, you must face reality when reconciling bank statements. (Wasted resources are hard to ignore when looking at your books.) Taking on that project was a choice, so you'll need to decide whether what you gained was worth what you gave up.

## Your Wellness Is Your Wealth

Of course, the cost of busyness shows up in other ways too. Though I pushed away the concept of wealth for too many years, I'm no longer willing to undervalue resources like my talent, time, energy, and money. Our society treats our wellness as an afterthought, but this is a deep-seated pattern I'm committed to disrupting—certainly in my own life, but also in the way I support my clients.

Many business decisions aren't inherently good or bad, but there *are* choices that are right or wrong for you and your goals. If you're not paying enough attention to your energy, consider this your nudge to find compassion for yourself. If your mission and your income are in direct conflict, something needs to shift. Chances are your body has been telling you the same thing, so stop overlooking these signals. I'm not saying it's easy to find a solution that pays the bills and makes a difference, but as a big-hearted entrepreneur, you must give yourself the space to figure it out. Narrow the scope of your offering. Raise your prices. Develop a scholarship program that provides greater access to you, but with clear limits. Offer tiered pricing that meets your people where they are. Stop customizing every project.

Delegate. There are countless ways to earn profit and nurture your mission. You need energy to bring your unique mission to the world.

## Opportunity or Obligation?

I've come up with a trusty way to decide whether to move forward with something. I ask myself, "opportunity or obligation?" In the past, my default was to assume a potential collaboration, partnership, or invitation was an opportunity. Psyched someone thought to include me, I tended to jump right in. Now, I've learned not to get carried away so fast. Anything that requires your time, energy, or money can fall into either camp. Slow down and discern which it is for you—right here, right now. The distinction depends on your own timing and current goals. In fact, something may be an obligation now but an opportunity later, or vice versa.

Caring humans like us have a hard time protecting the limits we've set for ourselves, but nurturing our energy is part of the job. Individuals who ask for our time may mean well. Maybe they're even doing work we admire. Often, we legitimately want to take on the new opportunity. But that doesn't mean now is the right time. Your inner wisdom will tell whether an invitation is right if you create enough space to listen. As we develop the habit of discernment, we get better at assessing these situations quickly. These days, any time someone asks me to ignore my instincts or sacrifice my energy, I turn the "opportunity" down and send it on its way.

The next time you're pondering whether to take on something new, pause before responding. Look inward.

**You get to decide what your priorities are.** Even if what you need seems selfish, you have the right to stand up for it.

Will it drain your energy? Before you say yes, make sure the answer feels good in your body. Productivity culture crops up in small ways we barely even notice, such as how we talk to ourselves. In her book *Set Boundaries, Find Peace: A Guide to Reclaiming Yourself*, licensed therapist Nedra Glover Tawwab warns entrepreneurs to pay attention. "I know that you consistently have work to do, but guess what? You're the boss, and you can define your limits." She says, "Avoid using phrases that are about working nonstop, such as 'hustle harder,' 'on the grind,' and 'rest later.'"

## Saying Yes to Everything? Say Goodbye to Impact

Saying yes is easy. The longer you've been conditioned to fill every gap, the harder it can be to say out loud, with no hesitation, "No." Even so, true leadership requires this skill. If you're agreeing to everything, your highest contribution will remain on hold.

We've all heard this before, but that doesn't mean we're good at saying no. Sometimes it's deeply uncomfortable. Other times, our agreement comes so readily we hardly even notice anything's wrong. (Once, I attended a local meetup just to check it out. By the end of the meeting, I'd become the group's secretary. Fortunately, I came to my senses the next day and politely declined. Upon reflection, I realized I hadn't even clicked with the group enough to want to return!)

In hustle culture, more is touted as better and there's lots of talk about how to maximize your time. But how often do we hear about managing our energy? Not nearly enough,

I say! There's no way around it: your energy has limits. With intention and action, you can retrain the guilt that kicks in every time you see a gap of need you could fill but shouldn't. Every task does not deserve an equal amount of your energy. Reserve your best for your true genius, for the mission that lights you up the most.

The next time you find yourself drained from doing too many things, remember this is a systemic construct you must reject. Follow the lead of Calvin Koon-Stack, director of foundation strategy at Spark Point Fundraising, who reminds staff to take care of themselves. (New employees tend to overdo it, developing unhealthy habits like not taking their vacation time.) "When you're in the mission-driven sector," he says, "you want to give your all and everything feels make-or-break, but this is not a healthy mindset for anyone to be productive in the long term. I've learned to appreciate the value of rest because taking a break can make us not only happier but also more effective. It shouldn't be a radical idea, but it clearly is."

Achieving your deepest impact requires rest. It requires space to think. It requires having enough energy to come up with solutions that aren't obvious. If you're still struggling with saying no, you could learn a thing or two from Cassandra Davis Speed, a member of my business networking group who runs an event center in Edina, Minnesota. She says, "Learn to say no in a *yes* way."

That might sound like, "Though I love the sound of your program, taking it on right now wouldn't allow me to partner with you in the wholehearted way we both deserve." Your unique mission is waiting, so it's worth making the effort to honor it.

I'd like to end this chapter with encouragement from one of my Twin Cities–based clients Cindy Karnes, founder of the Empowered Hours Club. She's one of the most energetic people I know, maybe in part because she's committed to valuing her energy. She cautions us all to pay attention when we sense something is off. "When you feel like you're pushing a mountain on your own, when things feel super hard, there's many different reasons, right?" she says. "But these awful feelings can be a clue that things are out of alignment." A variety of things could be off-kilter: a service based on dreaded tasks, a client that's not ideal, or even a messy workspace. Slow down, look around you, and do what it takes to align your energy with the outcomes you expect of yourself. As Karnes points out, the results are transformational. When the right things line up, she says, "it's like the weight of the world has left your shoulders. Momentum moves you forward and you become unstoppable!"

### ⓘ REFLECT

- Have you ever made a change that contributed to a feeling of unstoppable energy?
- Can you think of a time you made a decision you regretted because you were too busy to think straight?
- What do you think of the idea that constantly busy people are pushovers?

- What signals does your body send to let you know whether a decision is right or wrong for you?

- What is something big you want to achieve in your life that requires saying no to other things?

- How might it feel to accomplish that big thing?

## ☆ MAKE IT PRETTY

On a large piece of paper, create a table with two columns and several rows. Use a book or a ruler as your straight edge to draw the lines. Make each cell big enough for a phrase or sentence. Label the left column "Say No To" and the right column "Say Yes To." Fill in your rows right away or over time as ideas occur to you. Decorate the straight edges with washi tape from the craft store or your own doodles if you like.

## ♡ BRING IT TO LIFE

Say no to something this week. Make it a low-stakes activity or obligation, such as declining a phone call. Use the time to dream, even for five minutes.

# Make Time to Do the Most Good

"Do THE Most Good." This message is emblazoned on the wall at my beloved coworking space in St. Paul, Minnesota (it's called The Coven, and it lives up to its tagline as a community for radical changemakers). This huge pink tile installation sparks joy every time I see it, and the artistry of the space is a reason I chose it over the many hip coworking options in the Twin Cities.

As a big-hearted entrepreneur, doing good is how you're wired. It's how you see the world. The mission that calls you is always there, lurking in one form or another. On good days, you know you're empowering the people you're uniquely suited to serve. But for some of us, too many days are spent doing the piddly stuff while our highest contribution gets ignored.

In this chapter, I share how calendars can be a force for good—and full disclosure, I'm *not* a calendar person. Tight agendas make me twitch. I'd rather be in a state of flow than stick to a pre-set schedule.

For me, entrepreneurship has revealed the hard-won truth that the most valuable things I've done happened because I made time for them. The old cliché tells us time is money—and it ain't wrong!—but I'd like to add a corollary: time is impact.

Whether you're a planner nerd or a recovering calendar hater, here are some strategies I've found useful. They've increased time invested in my unique mission. I offer them as inspiration to mold in a way that works for you.

## Use Color to Prioritize Time

You've probably heard the expression "what gets measured gets done." This expression annoyed me at first, in the same way a step aerobics instructor can annoy you by being *way* too chipper. As a big-picture thinker, I have an underlying fear that a calendar system will box me in or choke my creativity and freedom.

After several years of trying it my way by avoiding calendar systems, I've come to know the wisdom of measuring time and I am now even an advocate for it. Thinking ahead and labeling my calendar with the categories I need to prioritize is integral to accomplishing my heftiest dream projects.

Case in point, while writing this paragraph I received two meeting requests for later this week. In the past, I would have agreed. But my calendar was already blocked to work on this manuscript, so I sent a link to my online scheduler and asked these people to find another time. Sure, I had my familiar pangs of guilt while saying no to their preference, but I've learned not to let that drive me. We don't owe everyone our time.

If you were to look at my Google calendar, you'd see at least eight colors indicating categories of activities:

- Sage for operations like marketing and finance
- Basil for content creation and dream projects
- Banana for clients
- Lavender for networking calls
- Grape for appointments, events, and professional development
- Tangerine for workshops I lead
- Flamingo for fun stuff
- Graphite for unassigned time

Are there other categories I could choose? Sure. Will other business owners need different categories to reflect their business model? Of course. What matters is that your categories support you in furthering your unique mission and ensure that your time is treated as an asset.

Without each of my categories, my business won't thrive and neither will I. They make it easy to assess the health of my venture at a glance. If the colors are balanced over the course of a month, I'm spending time effectively. I'm keeping the business running smoothly while maintaining my well-being. If one or more categories dominate my time, something's missing and I need to correct it.

The moment I enter something into my calendar, I like to apply a color to it. I also use a planner with prompts that encourage me to reassess things at the beginning of each week, month, and quarter. Doing a quick calendar check as often as possible at those times keeps me on track.

## Always Block Time for Your Next Dream Project

Your dreams aren't frivolous; they are just as valuable as your urgent tasks. Going after your ambitions will inspire others to do the same. You can use my calendar system to support you here.

I have blocked Mondays and Fridays indefinitely for Teach Your Thing development. I devote this time to whatever activities will move the needle on my business. Usually this includes two things: operations tasks and dream projects.

The first project I completed with these blocks was developing an online course that provided a slow but steady stream of passive income for four years. Reserving these days was an epic battle at first. For months, I forced it in—and even then, just barely. Over and over, this previously blocked time got obliterated by urgent tasks.

Still, I was determined to create that course, so I squeezed in whatever minutes I could, even if it meant only an hour or two on a given Monday or Friday. Weaning myself off other activities to honor this time triggered relentless guilt about what I wasn't doing. Day after day, my course creation efforts felt woefully insufficient. But gradually, the slices of time added up. After many months I looked back

**Your dreams aren't frivolous**—they're just as valuable as urgent tasks, and going after them will inspire others to do the same.

and the course was complete. Had I not blocked the days in advance, these moments never would have happened. The structure gave me the courage to start saying no to less impactful things I'd have automatically prioritized before. And guess what? I've since found that completed projects breed more completed projects.

My hope for you is that you start, wherever you are. Choose one project you want to dig into. Even if it's big or scary, determine what the appropriate amount of time to dedicate to it might look like for you. Choose a color that makes you happy or shows you mean business. Then, block it on your calendar from now until the end of time. Give yourself permission to do this. Think about how it will feel to get it done. Your highest contribution depends on it.

And though self-regulation isn't always fun, start chipping away at it, week by week.

## Leave Space for Unscheduled Stuff

I've been amazed at how much better I feel—and perform as a business owner—when there's honest-to-God space in my schedule. For a week to count as a good one, it must have time blocks that are completely blank. Does it always happen? No. But when I fill this time, I make sure there's evidence that time invested in that task will reap rewards down the road.

Before becoming self-employed, I dreamed of having space to respond to nature. Hey, every entrepreneur has their reasons for going it alone! So now, if it's a sunny June day, I'm determined to walk my golden retriever, Indy, once or twice a day. (As a Minnesotan who endures punishing winters, not relishing summer feels criminal.) Unscheduled time gives my day enough margin to choose when that happens. I never get tired of this benefit, which actively contributes to my well-being, sense of agency, and ability to strategize.

Some leaders I know schedule their breaks, like afternoon walks. If you're a calendar lover, go for it. For me, this feels too much like being told what to do. Though I'm the first to advocate for self-care as a business practice, designating slots for it has never worked for me. I'm highly motivated by inspiration. If there's unplanned space on my agenda, chances are good I'll choose a healthy way to use it. If I squander the time by doomscrolling, a clear sign I'm frazzled, I give myself grace. Tomorrow I'll exercise, putter in the garden, or take Indy to a local lake.

When I protect this time, I am a happier partner and a more effective consultant. I sleep through the night and I rarely feel the dread of work uncreated. Though I wish I could say I no longer hit the walls of exhaustion I once considered normal, these bouts have at least become rare and short-lived.

## ⑦ REFLECT

- Is there something you want to do but constantly remove from your calendar?
- What's one thing you might stop doing, or do differently, to make space for a dream project?
- Is there a category you need or want to add to your calendar, but you don't feel you deserve it?
- Is an old rule for success holding you back from putting yourself first?
- Write a new rule for success related to prioritizing your time.

## ☆ MAKE IT PRETTY

For this activity, question the assumption that you don't have time. In the center of your page, draw a large outline of a hand (trace your own if you feel like it). Then, jot down the things you can control and the things you can't. Put the things you can control inside your hand; everything else goes outside. Any time you're feeling overwhelmed, revisit your drawing and choose one thing you can control. Take action on it.

> ### ♡ BRING IT TO LIFE
>
> What's a dream project you'd like to make room for? Block it on your calendar indefinitely before other things can fill up that space.
>
> Who might help you free up your time? Ask for their help. (No, really—ask for their help.)

# 9

# Choose Mission and Money

"THAT'S ADORABLE. You're so cute." A participant in one of my cohort programs used these words to describe the subtext she hears in people's responses when they find out she runs her own business. Although DEI educator Liz Dempsey Lee is a PhD, she constantly reminds herself and others that she shouldn't be shortchanged for her services.

Unfortunately, as a woman and longtime educator, she's no stranger to being undervalued for her work. After all, she was a classroom teacher for many years. As she points out, passion-driven workers often implicitly receive the message that they don't really need a salary that will support them and their family because they do the work out of the goodness of their hearts.

## Let Go of the Scarcity Mindset

As a big-hearted entrepreneur, you need to shed the scarcity mindset that keeps you small. Trusting your ability to create opportunity is a learned skill, so start practicing now.

Every human being has the right to direct where their talents get channeled. We all deserve to say no to continual overwork that puts our health at risk. We all need time to reflect, to choose the moves that will take us where we want to go. And let's be clear, doing the work of disruption and invention takes a lot out of us.

More than five years before launching our respective businesses, Shona Ramchandani and I worked at the Minnesota History Center together. She headed up the robust internship program that fed into departments across our institution, including the education division where I developed curricular materials and led teacher workshops.

We've both held on to vital skills we learned at that major institution, like the importance of encouraging civic dialogue, amplifying absent narratives, and teaching critical thinking skills. But there are some unhealthy norms that, if we didn't learn them there, were certainly fostered there—and we've had to let go of them. Chief among them are the limiting money beliefs that pervade nonprofits. "As a business owner coming from the nonprofit industrial complex, I had to recognize that mission and money don't have to be the opposite of each other. I'm trying to get away from the idea that they're mutually exclusive; they are certainly not, in my personal life or my business," Ramchandani says.

## A DISEMPOWERING CHOICE

**MISSION**
Help Others
"If you work from the heart, money shouldn't matter."

**MONEY**
Help Yourself
"The bottom line is all that matters."

Now, Ramchandani prioritizes making space and capacity to do her best work, an act that requires owning her right to do so. She enthusiastically encourages big-hearted entrepreneurs like you to "take certain things off your plate that no longer need you, whether that's your household or your business." In fact, Ramchandani made a bold move her former scarcity-minded self would never have allowed: she hired a chef to prepare healthy meals for herself and her husband on a weekly basis. Now, with this basic need met, she has more energy to focus on moving her business forward. By leaning into abundance, she's also building a microeconomy that hires other BIPOC- (Black, Indigenous, and People of Color) and woman-owned businesses that she believes in.

If retaining help triggers guilt for you, Ramchandani and I recommend you pick up Rachel Rodgers's *We Should All Be Millionaires*. As Rodgers points out, "Strong women like us routinely forfeit our independence, our time, our power, and our success. We tolerate bullshit and feel guilty advocating for our own needs in our homes, at work, and in our national politics." She also points out that if you don't want to exploit low-income workers, don't. Pay a good living wage, offer flexible schedules, give people time off, and treat them well.

## Build an Abundance Mindset into Your Culture

A healthy mindset doesn't just happen, it takes intention. Especially if you've come from a fear-based environment, building a culture of opportunity for your customers or clients, your staff, and yourself will be transformative. Being a big-hearted entrepreneur "requires an attitude of abundance," says Calvin Koon-Stack of Spark Point Fundraising. "If you want to give of yourself, you must feel like you have a lot to share. We see a lot of our nonprofit clients operate from a scarcity mindset where they feel that resources are limited and time is tight, especially when compared to the big intractable problems they're trying to solve in the world. When you're looking at the number of resources you might have compared to the mission you want to achieve, it can be very intimidating."

He goes on, "The way we marry mission and money comes down to telling our staff how much we value them, as in, 'You've achieved so much for us. We want to return some of that investment to you.' That starts changing the mindset people have in the workplace."

Spark Point doesn't just talk this talk. I know because they hired me to develop an operations manual that lays out their processes. They defined their values in the first section of the manual because these principles serve as guidelines for everything they do. As I interviewed team members to capture their standard operating procedures, it became clear that this restorative culture is infused through workflows with internal and external stakeholders.

"As a business, we are able to compensate people relatively well. And that's, of course, wonderful. People have to pay their bills," says Koon-Stack. But the company takes the idea of abundance further. "We want to support our team members to live healthy, balanced lives. Many things go into that, including paid parental leave, a fully remote work environment, and generous vacation time, but those resources aren't helpful if people feel too busy to take a break. In quarterly reviews with my staff, I check in and ask, 'How have you been feeling these past three months? Do you have too much work? Do we need to move things off your plate? Have you used your vacation time?' Those conversations can be enlightening for me and my staff when we start talking about barriers to rest and tactically discussing how to delegate and prepare for rest." Spark Point is a living example of what can happen when a company owns its mission from the start, then continually invests in it.

## Navigate Your Pricing Sweet Spot

As a big-hearted entrepreneur, you need to figure out how to own your value while meeting your customers' needs. Business models vary widely in today's niche marketplace,

**Let go of any scarcity mindset** that keeps you small.

so expect to test and iterate as you create yours. Finding what works for you takes time, and evolution is part of the process. One option to consider is tiered pricing, with packages that can be scaled up or down for different levels of affordability.

In the case of my learning strategy business, I've found it helpful to provide a few levels of a base service. For example, people can come to Teach Your Thing for coaching as they build their workshop or course, or they can hire me to create content for it. Building tiered offerings may sound obvious, but I've devoted considerable time and energy to ensuring my packages meet clients where they are while also keeping my business scalable. One of my pet peeves is the prevalence of online service providers who breathlessly claim, "Double your prices, now double them again! You are abundant and worth it!" While I agree with the last part—oh yes—I have a fundamental problem with catering only to wealthy clients. But as someone who also learned the hard way that charging too little serves no one, I've landed on tiered structures as my solution. You know your business best, so pay close attention to what's not working for you. The sooner you can name the problem—in my case, it was too much customizing—the sooner you can find a better way to operate.

Algernon Hall, founder of Jubilee Children's Entertainment, provides assemblies, parent engagement workshops, and professional development to schools, from pre-kindergarten through to grade 12. Through high-energy school programs, he and his team motivate students and teachers to embrace their own genius, communicate effectively, and resolve conflict. Hall provides base programs that schools can customize if their budget allows.

"Some districts are larger than others. Some charter schools have a lot of money, some don't," he says, sharing how owning your worth can take time. "You're going to get undercut. Stepping out, I sent a quote for $3,000 for two assemblies. The guy asked me to give him a deal for $2,500. I was frustrated in a sense, but I came to a crossroads: When do I tell him no? For $500? Or do I totally walk away from $2,500? I moved ahead with it because I was trying to get into the district. But if he had said $1,500, I wouldn't have done it."

When I quote a price or settle a contract, I pay attention to how it feels in my body. On two occasions in my early days, I listened to advice from people who recommended dramatically increasing my price. At the time, I tried it on proposals without exploring why. Doing this brought dread into my stomach, but I moved forward anyway. In both cases, the prospect walked away with no response. I'm not saying the price was the definitive problem; perhaps this was a client mismatch that wouldn't have worked regardless. Even so, my inner wisdom was on track. Something wasn't right and I knew it. A similar icky feeling also occurs when I quote a number that's below my worth. Any time I move forward with a devalued price, resentment haunts me throughout the project. The opportunity costs add up. There's nothing like a low-paying project to reveal the many things you could be doing to bring about a better return.

Now, any time I feel dread related to my pricing, I take it as a clue that I need to adjust something, usually price point, scope, or both. Over time, I've also streamlined my process and built packages because constant customization is exhausting and confusing.

Simply put, passion-driven business owners need to find their sweet spot. Nobody's saying it's easy to build relationships, open the door to opportunity, and generate profit at the same time. As you go, channel this encouragement from Hall: "Find that sweet spot you're comfortable with, but also keep in mind what your value is."

> ### ⑦ REFLECT
>
> - What's one word that characterizes your mindset about charging for your time and expertise?
>
> - Your business is its own microeconomy. Who do you want it to support?
>
> - When you quote your pricing, how does it feel in your body?
>
> - Is there something about your offer you'd like to adjust, like price, tiers, or scope?
>
> - How can you treat yourself with compassion when navigating both mission and money?

## ☆ MAKE IT PRETTY

Make an attractive quote board to help you replace limiting beliefs. (A utilitarian whiteboard won't do!) My office features one I made: a large wooden frame with fabric behind the glass. Using a dry-erase marker, I write messages on it that inspire me, often from whatever business book I'm reading at the time. Right now my board features a statement made by the facilitator of a course I'm taking for women entrepreneurs: "Girlfriend, you are not a flea market."

## ♡ BRING IT TO LIFE

Apply an empathy map (see opposite page) to your beliefs. Rethink an old rule of success that may be holding you back. Write it down at the bottom left of the map under the heading "Old Rule of Success." For example, "You work from the heart, so money shouldn't matter." Fill out the top four sections of the empathy map.

- What am I **hearing** about this rule? (For example, "You're an educator? Good luck making a living!" "Social entrepreneurs can't run a real business." "Doing good is just a marketing ploy.")

- What am I **seeing**? (For example, news stories of billionaires with large egos or mission-driven people who struggle to pay the bills.)

- What am I **thinking and feeling**? ("I'm in a helping profession, so all that matters is making a difference." "I'm too busy to think about my retirement savings right now." "Wealth is unattainable for someone like me.")

- What am I **saying and doing** as a result? (Saying: "Is my work good enough?" Doing: Procrastinating on my budget.)

- On the bottom right, empower yourself by rewriting the rule. (For example, "I combine mission and money to thrive in today's economy.")

**EMPATHY MAP**

| THINK AND FEEL | SEE |
|---|---|
| HEAR | SAY AND DO |
| Old rule of success | My new version |

# 10

# Pay Attention to Your Wealth

THERE'S NO way around it: if you want to bring your deepest mission to the world, you must face your money issues. Far too many of my big-hearted friends resist focusing on their finances. They know this is a problem, but they're so busy doing other things that they hesitate to address it. To you and them I say, "Start paying attention to your wealth." Nobody should care about it more than you. In *The Soul-Sourced Entrepreneur*, Christine Kane reminds us we have more control than we think: "When you 'pay attention' to something, you're literally giving—spending, disbursing, investing—a highly valuable resource: your power." She goes on to say, "In the twenty-first century, the phrase 'paying attention' is for real. You are that powerful. But the players in the Attention Economy are betting on you not understanding that. They're counting on the ease with which you'll hand over your attention to their agendas."

Handing over our attention means ceding control over any aspect of our wealth, whether it's our talent, our inner knowing, our energy, or our time. In this chapter, I'll focus on the aspect we tend to avoid the most: money.

## Notice Your Money Fears

When I conducted interviews for this book, I was shocked to discover that a powerhouse client of mine had once been plagued by money fears. When Mindy Martell hired me to turn her methodology into an online education program, she'd been in business for twenty years. She runs Clothier Design Source, an apparel factory and design house in St. Paul, Minnesota. Martell, along with her ninety employees, has helped more than a thousand microbrands make hundreds of thousands of products.

Her big-hearted mission has three parts: teaching entrepreneurs to succeed, encouraging sustainable and socially responsible practices through US-made products, and getting people to take her industry seriously. After all, apparel production is *engineering*, not just sewing. A proactive advocate for small businesses, Martell goes against the grain of an industry that caters to huge players, often with little transparency.

So, I was floored to discover Martell had once struggled with owning her worth. "I have a story about undercharging way back in the beginning, and beyond that, collecting payment. Clients would come to me with new jobs and I'd be like, 'Yeah, but you haven't paid me for the last one yet.' I had a really hard time saying it. I had a mentor at the time who made me role-play asking for my money. I remember bawling. I was like, 'I can't do it.'"

Many do-gooders have internalized some version of the belief that wealth isn't for us. We've been told to think charging for our gifts is selfish, or that marketing means shoving ourselves onto people who don't want us. We've bought into the idea that as creatives, we're not numbers people; that investments are complicated; or even that ambition itself looks ugly, especially on us.

## How Deeply Rooted Are Your Beliefs?

Entrepreneurship made me face the fact that reluctance to talk or think about money was rooted in my psyche. This ambivalence had become so normalized that it took me years to even notice it. I grew up in a middle-class family that valued stability and saving, but money itself was never a big topic in our household. Instead, we focused on how to be active contributors to our community in other ways. As young people who modeled our parents' example, my brother Michael and I chose careers as public servants: he became an Episcopal priest, and I became a museum educator. My mom and dad are models for what community engagement should look like. They instilled in us the values they foster as Christians, like loving your neighbor. (Of course, there are countless historic and modern examples of people using Christianity and other organized religions as a weapon or force for exclusion, but this is not the brand of spirituality my family supports.)

I'm hard-pressed to recall a single instance of being told to swear off wealth, but something tells me I adopted this notion early on. My fifteen-year career as a nonprofit employee heavily reinforced the idea that mission mattered above all else, and that expecting competitive wages was out of the question, laughable even. (Several years after I left my museum educator role at the Minnesota History Center, the employees established a formal staff union to campaign for fair pay and other rights. Go, brave souls, go!)

We all have our own assumptions about money. Maybe you were raised to believe money causes conflict or that it will solve all your family's problems. Maybe you associated it with a parent's love or lack thereof. Maybe you're convinced it changes people. The list goes on, but eventually, you'll have to stare your beliefs in the face. My entrepreneur friend and DEI facilitator Angele Goss wrestled with this contradiction: "I've struggled for a while with the question, 'Can you be a successful, income-earning entrepreneur and Christian at the same time?'" In the end, she realized these two parts of her identity could, in fact, live together. Mentors helped her see that there's a cost to her time, knowledge, and customization. Receiving validation when she charges more has helped her "push to that next level." Most importantly, it has expanded the places she can reach with her facilitation of difficult, but much-needed, dialogue about equity, authenticity, and collaboration.

## Rewrite the Beliefs That Hold You Back

Only you know whether your own relationship with money is good for the health of your business. If you've been blocking your ability to generate income, it's worth digging into the root cause. And if you're concerned compassion will weaken your profits, it's time to rethink those old rules of success. This deep work can help you make better decisions, adopt healthier habits, and multiply your impact.

If you need to rewrite beliefs you've lived with for a long time, consider recording your thoughts in a journal. Initially, I had a hard time shedding the messages I'd taken on as a nonprofit museum educator. So, I sat down one day and wrote new stories I wanted to adopt. At the time they were entirely aspirational; now, I have evidence to show that my updated beliefs are, in fact, valid:

- Money amplifies good work.

- Wealth will help me improve communities in ways I can't yet imagine.

- Education is needed in any business, and it's a superpower worth paying for.

- I'm just as capable, if not more so, than plenty of people making good money.

- Unleashing my creativity, strategy, and skill will provide me with new ways to make money.

- Work can and should make use of the talents that light me up, at least a good portion of the time.
- To make money, I need to take care of myself.

It wasn't until my mid-40s that I discovered "wealth" isn't a bad word. For as long as I could remember, I saw income solely as an exchange for hard work. Thanks to becoming a business owner, I finally grasped the concept that my assets—time, energy, and money—could multiply. Even now, I confess that on some level the thought still blows my mind.

In my employee days, I did have a 401(k), but I saw retirement accounts as far off, inaccessible, and confusing. My employers did little to show us workers otherwise, as their attention was focused on the institutional mission.

## Recognize Systemic Disparity

For most of my adult life, I've felt intimidated by the financial services industry. I had few interactions with professionals, and the ones I did have left me feeling awkward, disempowered, and angry. Many advisors I researched had policies that made it clear my net worth as a museum educator wasn't worth their time. The consequences were disastrous and long-term. When I did finally hire a financial advisor, he later went to prison for defrauding me and at least twenty others out of our nest eggs. He rolled my retirement fund into an account he controlled, then spent it himself. The theft occurred in my mid-40s, and yes, the

If you are new to understanding money, **it's time to talk about it, manage it, and earn more of it.**

experience was as devastating as it sounds. Money I'd saved for more than twenty years was gone instantly. While I later received about 15 percent of the amount back—my portion of the restitution for victims—the loss of the rest left a crater in my future plans and sense of security.

But here's the thing. As alarming as my story is, I'm hardly alone in having a hard relationship with money. Financial ignorance is common (and understandable) for a whole host of reasons. I have no doubt that you have stories of your own. But if I have anything to say about it, you won't have to sit in a federal courtroom and watch a judge hand your financial advisor a seven-year sentence. Take it from me: nobody has more of a right to your wealth than you do. That's right—nobody.

Encouraging big-hearted changemakers to get right with money is a big part of why I wrote this book. But the topic is nuanced, so let me try to explain. Surviving this crime has been gut-wrenching and ongoing, but in the same breath I feel compelled to acknowledge that I am the beneficiary of established systems that hold others back unfairly. We live in a culture of racism, gender binaries, and other unjust structures. As a white, cisgender individual, I feel safe most of the time. Thanks to family support, I've never had to wonder where my next meal was coming from, even after the theft. When I enter a public space, I'm viewed favorably by peers and authority figures. I can attend business events without feeling outnumbered, and I'm never asked to speak for all members of my race. I'm protected from the kind of harm that is often turned on people of color, and I've never had to hide my identity at work. I can't take for granted that my mom and dad taught me the value of saving from a young age, or that they sent me to college.

Despite these advantages, I also spent decades believing that wealth is problematic and not for me. As a woman and an educator, I received subtle and direct messages telling me there were limits to what I should achieve. I learned firsthand that hierarchies can be damaging and that glass ceilings are real. "We [women] are taught that our financial goals are too big and that we are inadequate to accomplish them," Rachel Rodgers says in *We Should All Be Millionaires*. But as she also points out, "only in the last hundred years have laws been passed to stop widespread discrimination against women's economic lives."

Systemic disparity leads to internalized shame, and challenges to our prosperity come in many forms. I was once told by a woman in leadership that men taking credit for our work is simply how it is. If I wanted to move up, she said, I needed to get over it, as she herself had done for years. Now, I'm convinced we can't make change if we're afraid to talk about uncomfortable things. No matter what form our wealth comes in—time, talent, energy, and especially money—it's a triggering topic, and for good reason. But avoiding talking about wealth weakens our impact.

As politician and lawyer Stacey Abrams says in *Lead from the Outside*, "Women and people of color are typically viewed as beggars at the table, not the bankers behind the desk." Indeed, as she says, "money can be a crippling obstacle to power and leadership."

No wonder taking ownership over our prosperity requires intention and resilience. If you are new to understanding money for whatever reason, it's time to talk about it, manage it, and earn more of it. But don't expect to do this on your own. Finding people you trust to help you overcome financial roadblocks is fundamental. Your wealth allies are out there. But it's up to you to seek them out thoughtfully, in a way that empowers you. Hiring the wrong financial advisor cost me dearly. As a crime survivor I'm not to blame, but I'll never again be hands off about money or professional services.

## Find Your Wealth Allies

If you don't consider yourself a money person, my advice is to get clear about what you need help with. Especially when you're seeking support from financial professionals, you should accept nothing less than those who actually meet the needs you've defined.

I made a point of seeking out a bookkeeper and a CPA who are open to my questions, never rushing me or making me feel silly for asking. When I needed a lawyer to review a contract, I got recommendations from small-business owners who are creatives like me. The research paid off. Though I was dreading the experience, this attorney treated me like a human being rather than a billable hour. She also empowered me by teaching me things I'd never considered.

The more unfamiliar you are with the task at hand, the more important it is to interview a few professionals and not just go with the first one who comes your way. Pay attention to how you feel while interacting with them. Do they listen to your concerns? If they get testy or defensive when you ask questions, they're not helping you. Even if financial professionals come from a world you don't know, keep in mind that they work for you, not the other way around. They may be the expert in their field, but no one knows more about your money's true value than you.

My client Laina Latterner also discovered the value of hiring the right professionals. When seeking legal help, she started by calling someone she trusted. She engaged their institution for an initial process but "something didn't sit right." She had an uneasy feeling and couldn't put her finger on why.

"It took me three months to take action," she says. Despite her desire to move forward, her inner compass refused to steer her wrong. "Logically, I went through my corporate brain and said, 'All this makes sense on paper.' But in my gut, it still didn't." The firm was large and well known, but they offered only one clear path forward: theirs. Throughout the process, Latterner rarely felt heard. Some of their recommendations didn't even align with her business needs.

In the end, she hired another firm, independently referred to her by two businesswomen in her network. This time, she had no doubt. The new company catered to small-business owners. Listening to and respecting her philosophy, they articulated solutions that reflected her values and made sense for her goals. "It took me three months to get my legal stuff in order, which cost me money," Latterner concludes, "but it was the right move for me. If you find someone who doesn't fully support you, it's gonna be a lot harder than it already is."

## Build a More Human Economy

If we want to contribute to a wider movement, we must start at a personal level. Opening ourselves to new possibilities is part of the process. And we must take a stand. After all, according to community-driven economic strategists Jess Rimington and Joanna Levitt Cea, "The lovelessness of the current economic system is perpetuated mostly by people who consider themselves to be playing by its rules." In Rimington and Levitt Cea's book, *Beloved Economies: Transforming How We Work*, they assert that shaping a new, more human economy is possible. They share their extensive research on organizations that have found bold ways to break out of business as usual.

"Even though the system is currently rigged in favor of those with consolidated wealth, it is also true that systemic change can be powerfully sparked at the grassroots level by individuals and enterprises joining together," they note.

As big-hearted business owners, we have a special and powerful role to play. Our money is a crucial asset—much like our time, talent, and energy. Taking ownership of our wealth is a necessary step toward building the world we want for ourselves and our communities. In part two, I'll talk about what it means to look outward and find ways to engage others in the dialogues that matter.

## ⓘ REFLECT

- How well are you paying attention to your money right now?
- As a big-hearted entrepreneur, what fears do you have around money?
- What cultural beliefs about money have you had in the past? What do you believe now?
- Have you experienced systemic injustice related to wealth?
- Is trying to live up to others' financial status causing you stress, guilt, or shame?
- What did your family of origin teach you about money?
- What emotions might affect your ability to run a business with confidence and ease?

## ☆ MAKE IT PRETTY

Journal about a money issue that's provoking fear, shame, or guilt. Choose one or two emotions you'd rather feel instead. Use watercolors, colored pencils, or markers to highlight the emotions. Then, write about three things you can do to address the concern, like hiring help or making time to develop a new product that could scale your business.

## ♡ BRING IT TO LIFE

Identify a few trusted allies who might be open to having regular conversations about money. They could be family members, friends, colleagues, or hired professionals. Reach out and set up a time and place that's mutually convenient. Go deep. Talk about the actions you're taking and planning, and your limiting emotions or mindsets. Share resources on finances and investing and talk about ways you might become accountability buddies.

PART TWO

# AMPLIFY A MISSION THAT MATTERS

IN THE second half of this book, we explore the outward stuff of being an entrepreneur: amplifying a mission that matters. Business is a powerful tool for starting meaningful dialogue and propelling people into action. If you want to make change, you need to arrange your ideas and make containers for distributing them. And as big-hearted leaders know, generating solutions means staying in community. Now more than ever, you need to ditch perfection and focus instead on connection.

# 11

# Embrace Authenticity over Perfection

I GREW UP believing that if I wanted to succeed at something, I had to get things right. To do this, I listened to instructions, paid attention to what was expected of me, and followed the rules. Mistakes meant carelessness and were to be avoided at all costs.

The truth is perfectionism holds us back—and it's a societal construct we can reject. As I've come to know, it's also a gilded invitation to silence. (Oh, the allure of faultlessness.) If we buy into the notion, knowingly or subconsciously, that we shouldn't share our work until it's flawless, we miss out on opportunities to be leaders. Yet too many of us, especially women, spend time with our heads down, tinkering with our words and ideas and even our looks, hoping we'll present ourselves just as others want to see us. As Tara Mohr points out in *Playing Big: Practical Wisdom for*

*Women Who Want to Speak Up, Create, and Lead,* "years of that conditioning leaves many adult women looking for the next degree or book or few hours of research to give them the answers they need for whatever task is before them. Yet playing big often requires the opposite: *accessing what we already know, trusting its value, and bringing it forth.*"

Fortunately, Mohr also teaches us to unlearn these old habits. The strategies she recommends are right on, such as telling our own story and creating with our intended audience in mind instead of quietly in a room by ourselves. I've used these strategies in my own business, and although they make me feel vulnerable, they consistently lead to results. Mohr's book also includes one of my favorite quotes of all time. If you attend one of my workshops, you may see it on a slide: "Everything in your life has led you to this moment. Right here, right now. You are meant to be here. What you have to say needs to be said. There are so many people who need to hear your message and just the way you need to say it. This is your sacred work. Do not go home. Walk into that room and claim your space."

Yes, Tara, yes! In a world that tells us big-hearted entrepreneurs that our work isn't possible, we can't hear this message enough.

### Your Voice Has Power, So Use It

Owning a business is one of the best ways to use your voice—and yet, to do it well, you need to reconcile the hang-ups you may have about looking or sounding a certain way. Your people want to hear from you as you really are.

I learned this lesson in my early days of entrepreneurship as I gained the courage to publish my first online course. It's called The Empowered Presenter, and it teaches introverts how to embrace public speaking.

At the time I didn't have a course platform (or even a website), so I decided to post my course on Skillshare, a learning community for creatives that hosts thousands of classes. But when I conducted a quick field study of the options already on the site, I got slammed with imposter syndrome. I was so intimidated that I nearly gave up right then.

"How could my class possibly measure up to these?" I panicked. "Who do I think I am? It's not like I'm Tony Robbins!" One class particularly spooked me. It was taught by a guy who'd built a business around training employees to give talks. He was confident and well spoken, and his case studies showed a track record with well-known companies.

Fortunately, one of my mentors helped me overcome this fear. His name is Stephen Warley, and he took me on as a beta client for his coaching business and podcast, *Life Skills That Matter*. I told him I'd seen the competition and no longer wanted to develop this course. I said, "Now that I've seen what's out there, my idea seems silly."

He wasn't content to let me throw away the plan. "That other course may be good," he nudged me, "but it doesn't have *your voice*. It was made by a millennial man, right? You said he's confident and polished. Will he appeal to people? Yes, of course. There's a subset out there who want to learn from him."

What Warley said next changed the course of my brand forever. "But plenty of people won't respond to him. They'd rather learn from a Gen X woman who openly talks about

You can create safe spaces. And if you want to change your community for the better, **the spaces you build must also be brave.**

what it feels like to be nervous. In today's niche marketplace, your job is to find those people and connect with them."

We ended our video call, and I recommitted to my plan. I spent the next month-and-a-half making the class. And you know what happened? The process of developing it—breaking down steps, writing activities, and creating video lessons—reinforced my confidence. I did, in fact, know what I was talking about! More importantly, I had something unique and valuable to say.

Soon after publishing the course, my learning strategy services took off. Because I got too busy with client work, I never cultivated a relationship with Skillshare. I spent no time marketing the class and I didn't add a single other piece of content to the platform. Even so, that class had a good run! In four years, it generated $1,200 of entirely passive income.

This money was never intended to be the backbone of my business, but it proved an undeniable point: even in a crowded marketplace, there is room for my point of view. And even if I didn't believe it before creating the class, I now have 1,191 students that prove its value. Together, they spent 22,339 minutes watching my material. I'm grateful I didn't let fear get in the way.

## Choose Authenticity over Perfection

When framing a conversation about something of deep importance to you, it can be easy to worry about exactly how you'll say it. Especially for high achievers who've been rewarded for doing things "right," getting started is a challenge in and of itself. Though growth brings pitfalls, avoiding it keeps us small. I'm not saying excellence doesn't matter; to the contrary, it is worth striving for—but it's not the same as perfection. Crafting ideas thoughtfully matters to me, so much so that it's a foundation of my brand. I get the sweats whenever someone suggests I try a social media platform designed for speed over quality. Still, strict adherence to flawlessness is not benign. It causes suffering and it prevents your solution, *your voice*, from reaching someone who needs it.

To share a message that matters, social entrepreneurs must take a stand. Often, this means speaking out against cultural beliefs that dominate your industry. Barb Buckner Suárez uses her birth education programming to let parents know they can trust themselves and put intimacy first, with each other and their children.

Expectations of foolproof parenting tend to monopolize Buckner Suárez's field, and she's fired up to change this outdated notion. "We're human beings being raised by human beings," she says, "so sometimes we fuck it up." Through parenting classes and her podcast *Birth Happens*, she lets parents know that "you don't have to be perfect at it. It's really about 'when I'm available to you, I'm attuning with you. And if I screw up, I come back and repair.' Those things can change literally generations of trauma."

Buckner Suárez is intentional about creating a safe space for her audience, and her style is authentic to her. "If you see me anywhere—in a presentation, in my podcast, on my blog, or in person—all those pieces are going to completely line up." To build trust and shatter illusions of superiority,

Buckner Suárez avoids using the word "expert" on her website. Yes, she's experienced—for over twenty-five years, she has supported thousands and thousands of pregnant folks and their partners. But she prefers to call herself a guide: "I put myself out there as a hiking guide or somebody you could sit down and have a beer with. I had a former mom in one of classes say, 'She's like a cool aunt,' and I thought, 'That's exactly what I want to be.'"

Though not all of us can pull off cool, every big-hearted entrepreneur should strive to create safe spaces where people can be themselves. (Note that if you are in the majority, safety for you may not mean safety for all.) And if you want to change your community for the better, the conversations you facilitate must be brave too.

## Create Safe, Brave Spaces

To amplify her own mission, educator Liz Dempsey Lee is also intentional about creating learning experiences that foster both security and courage. Committed to getting white and white-adjacent people to talk about systemic injustice, she says, "We all benefit from grappling with problems in a safe and comfortable environment, one that's set up to allow you to make mistakes, or even to fail, and then to pick yourself up and try it again. So that's one thing I bring forward in terms of education. I also really believe in storytelling and hands-on activities, especially when you're talking about things like diversity, equity, and inclusion."

By creating a container for her audience to engage in gritty conversations, Dempsey Lee is a living example of a quote from one of my favorite business leaders, community builder Pamela Slim. Slim continually advocates for bringing humanity to business. Whenever I get stuck in fear around how to say something challenging or painful, I consult my journal for a note I took during one of her talks: "Be transactional with systems and relational with people."

As you amplify your unique mission, don't attack anyone personally. But when it comes to dismantling systems, big-hearted entrepreneurs should seek the courage to say what needs to be said. You won't do it perfectly; that's not possible, especially when a subject is complex and important. When you're in a community, your people can help improve your message. They ask questions that make you think, they challenge you with new perspectives, and they cheer you on when you're afraid.

## ⓘ REFLECT

- How does imposter syndrome show up for you as a mission-driven leader?
- What unique voice do you bring to debates in your industry?
- Is there something you want to create, but you've convinced yourself that someone else's voice is more valuable than your own?

- What can you do to create a safe, brave space for meaningful dialogue in your community?

## ☆ MAKE IT PRETTY

As you consider starting a dialogue about a problem you want to solve, give yourself permission to let go of the solutions for now. Instead, start with the questions. Get out your journal and draw a giant question mark on the page. Set a timer for five minutes and generate as many questions as you can about this societal issue. Jot down whatever comes to mind, including questions your audience might have and ones you have yourself. Let the questions help you generate ideas for when, where, or how to facilitate a conversation that might move the needle.

## ♡ BRING IT TO LIFE

Create something quickly—a two-sentence response to a news item or a fifteen-second video about a project you're working on, a book you're reading, or one of your end-of-the-workday rituals. As soon as you create it, share it, whether that's on social media or with a client. Let your imperfect authentic voice be heard.

# 12

# Facilitate Dialogue
## (A.K.A. Avoid the Loathsome Cliché)

PART OF your role as a business owner is to facilitate meaningful conversations with your people. But what do you talk about, and how?

In the zeitgeist of small business, there's a belief that successful messaging means putting yourself out there (the loathsome cliché). This claim's promise of ease makes me cringe: "Just put yourself out there and the followers will find you, the buyers will come, and all will be well!"

As appealing as it may sound, this idea is misleading. Not because it's wrong per se, but because it is incomplete. When it comes to being influential—and turning profit—you cannot do it on your own. Putting yourself out there is a one-sided act. It's a transaction; no relationship required.

Every successful business owner I know builds relationships as part of their job. Inside and outside of their venture, they do a heck of a lot more than just put themselves out there. They've figured out how to listen and how to keep the conversation going over time.

I'd like to offer up a replacement phrase for "put yourself out there." If you're ready to heed the calling that's been nudging you, don't just put yourself out there—start facilitating dialogue.

### Get Out of Your Head!

The table on page 140 shows some key differences between putting yourself out there and facilitating dialogue. Ultimately, the distinction has to do with working in community versus working alone. You understand this, of course, but getting out of your head is another thing entirely.

The mission-driven business owners I know are highly adept at discussing the difficult problems they seek to solve. That said, talking publicly about complex issues is a legitimate challenge. We must address them in a way that's simple enough to inspire people to act but still allows us to run profitable ventures.

Many factors keep us from leading dialogues that encourage action, including overwhelm and imposter syndrome, not to mention the global problem of political extremism that enters public spaces both in person and online. Still, it's worth our time to identify the conversations that we can lead meaningfully. For me, doing this relates directly to the internal work of owning my value.

The better we know ourselves, the faster we can let go of the idea that we must host *all* the conversations and start facilitating the ones that light us up. The sooner we can show up in the forums that make sense for our unique goals and highest contribution, the better we'll be able to make a difference.

DEI consultant Angele Goss has built a career around hosting hard conversations. She amplifies her message by fostering a sense of community in every group she encounters, including corporate teams, nonprofit leadership groups, adult education classrooms, and small businesses. "I'm not afraid of the hard conversations," she says, not even the ones that "typically would be derogatory toward a woman or a woman of color. I'm not emotionally triggered by comments that people might have as they're trying to figure this out."

Goss focuses on what lights her up: the individuals she serves. "I want each person in a group to be recognized as a whole person," she says.

One group she serves is adult basic education students, who are not usually native English speakers. "My students are from all over the globe. I try to really allow their place in the world to be amplified. I ask them where they're from and I ask them to bring in their cultural perspectives, because that's something you don't typically get an opportunity to do in American classrooms."

Any business owner can learn from Goss's example. Sure, her professional training adds to her value proposition, but you don't have to be a paid facilitator to host meaningful dialogue. Keep in mind, too, that not all conversations happen in person. There are many ways to go about it, and most of the coming chapters cover options like social media, newsletters, events, and courses.

| PUT YOURSELF OUT THERE | FACILITATE DIALOGUE |
| --- | --- |
| Position yourself as an expert with all the answers. | Question your assumptions and invite hard conversations. |
| Think your business needs to address the entire problem you're trying to solve. | Focus on value-driven conversations that you can lead meaningfully. |
| Create programs and offerings alone, tinkering and overthinking. | Invite feedback from pilot participants, your audience, or a wider community. |
| Market and sell by pitching your knowledge and features. | Ask questions. Listen to what matters to your people, then invite them to buy. |
| Seek certainty. | Seek connection. |
| Think you have to figure it all out yourself. | Let your people shine. |
| Assume your staff and stakeholders know your values. | Be intentional about teaching your values. |
| Forget that your money can do the talking for you. | Take time to find vendors who support your values. |

## Question Your Assumptions

I met Molly Clark and Maddy Kaudy, the founders of Taking Stock Foods, at my St. Paul coworking space The Coven. They spent two years perfecting the recipes for their line of slow-cooked, certified organic bone broths. Their company is devoted to local growers, makers, and markets. And they're active voices in conversations about food production. Not content to stop there, Clark and Kaudy are also "clapping back at fatphobic messaging on social media by food brands."

It's this issue that led me to meet these founders. One day, while writing an early draft of this book, I was ready for a tea break. As I strolled from my cozy chair in the corner to the kitchen, I noticed a spread of healthy snacks on the community table. Surrounding the snacks was a small group of women, and one mentioned that an event was about to start. Clark and Kaudy were hosting a fifteen-minute listening session on fatphobia in wellness messaging and they asked if I'd like to participate.

I could tell right away the conversation would be meaningful, so I was thrilled to join. What followed was a series of questions about our experience with wellness messaging. No one in the group had met before, and our various industries and backgrounds led to multiple perspectives on the issue. (The conversation was so inclusive that I'm pretty sure we stuck around for forty-five minutes.)

Later, I was curious to discover what Clark and Kaudy had gleaned from the discussion. "A big lesson we learned is that our assumptions need to be questioned," says Clark. "We might just confirm our own bias by working through an idea with our inner circle. I have a strong working knowledge of how fatphobia connects to wellness, but through the session I found out that I need to introduce folks to this connection as it is not common knowledge at this time."

Whenever you lead conversations about your values, **remember that you don't have to push your ideas onto others.**

Though I didn't ask how much prep time the session took, I'd guess the meeting was relatively easy to set up. Kudos to these women for gaining a high return on their time investment; they gained valuable insight from a single conversation.

Their question-driven approach is an admirable model to follow. Whenever you lead conversations about the values that matter to you, remember that you don't have to push your ideas onto others. In fact, long-winded pitching is an old-school carryover from the mass market economy. Under that traditional model, sellers tend to push their product or service with less consideration about what value it offers to the customer or client. But our marketplace has changed. It caters to niches, which are infinite and driven by purpose, personality, and uniqueness. To attract their own niche, today's big-hearted leaders need to adopt a strategy of collaborative conversations that guide buyers to a confident purpose.

## Seek Connection, Not Certainty

Jason Jones of The Coaching Hour built a business around helping coaches and salespeople embrace this new world by letting go of the dated sales pitch. He and his clients have found success and ease in sales by asking questions.

"There's so much emphasis on 'Let me tell you what I know and that I'm an expert,'" Jones points out. "And that just overwhelms people." His interactive workshop series, Adaptive Conversations for Conscious Sales, helps clients develop questions instead. Jones guides his participants to identify the needs and problems they solve for their clients. They write five or six questions related to those needs and are then assigned the task of asking people these questions. Along the way, they learn to reshape their mindset. Rather than seeking certainty, their goal is to find clarity.

"If you're pursuing clarity," Jones argues, "you're pursuing understanding what's really happening, what's going on in the reality of this person right now." Clarity provides a more successful outcome than certainty. "If we're trying to be certain, that means we're trying to validate what we think and know about the person."

What's key about this distinction? "Certainty and validation take us away from connection," Jones says. And for big-hearted business owners, connection is everything. The skill of cultivating dialogue will serve you well in every aspect of your business, from sales to client work to relationship-building in your community. Later chapters in this book cover specific containers you can use to amplify your unique mission. Start considering ones that might work for you as you explore ways to lead meaningful conversations.

## ⓘ REFLECT

- What does it mean to you to facilitate dialogue rather than put yourself out there?
- How can you test your assumptions about a viewpoint you feel strongly about?
- Name one way you've sought certainty rather than connection. What would it look like to seek connection instead?
- How can you stay true to your core values when someone in your community (or outside of it) disagrees with you?

## ☆ MAKE IT PRETTY

Reimagine the table on page 140. Draw two columns in your journal, one labeled "Put Myself Out There" and one called "Facilitate Dialogue." Create rows with enough space to write. Use colorful pens to fill in how you might show these distinctions in your work. Be specific. Name things you've done in the past or want to do in the future.

## ♡ BRING IT TO LIFE

Create a short poll for your people. Post it on social media.

# 13

# Cultivate Warm Connections

WHEN YOU hear the word "networking," what comes up for you? You may be naturally relational, but you're probably also familiar with the cringe that comes with traditional networking events (or even the idea of them). Far too many of us consider networking to be exclusionary, empty exchanges meant to serve certain people in a one-sided, pushy way.

This outmoded, unappealing way of thinking doesn't cut it anymore. When you have a purpose above and beyond the bottom line, your work happens with and for those you serve. (You probably already see your business as a resource in your own community, at least on some level.) Use my trusted practice to find your people and connect with them quickly by making meaningful relationships based on shared values.

## Let Your Purpose Take the Lead

The method on pages 150 to 154 shows how I started my business in the first place, but I later formalized it as an exercise for a workshop I led at a job transition group. A prime time to use it is when you're establishing a new program and are seeking beta participants for feedback, but it's also meant to maximize your networking overall.

The goal is to get beyond the standard introduction of "My name is Suzi. I create education experiences, so buy my stuff." Instead, you'll introduce yourself by asking a compelling question about the mission you stand for.

Each time I lead this activity at a workshop, the room's energy palpably shifts when people introduce themselves. People chime in with points of connection. Animated conversations spark organically as people shoot up from their seats to meet each other, remaining well after the scheduled ending time. More than once, people reached out afterward to tell me they got a job or a new type of lead they'd never considered.

## Don't Sell Yourself—Build Community

When you launch a new offering or create a piece of content, you may think about reaching a bunch of strangers, forgetting that you already have warm connections. Some of these people know and trust you, and others are new but already care about your mission. These folks are more likely to engage with you without having to be coaxed into a dialogue.

When I developed the original service offerings for Teach Your Thing, I wanted to amplify the message that education is powerful, but I wasn't sure just how my instructional design skills could help the businesses I wanted to serve. I needed to hear from real people, but I was new to entrepreneurship and didn't have many business leaders in my network—or so I thought at first.

Before contacting anyone, I began with my purpose. As a museum educator, I'd known for decades that education changes the world, but now I was combining this idea with my newfound love of entrepreneurship. My goal was to identify small-business owners who shared these dual passions and who would embrace a conversation about how education content could help them increase their impact. Not just anyone would do; the conversations had to be mutually beneficial and capable of cultivating warm connections.

If you were to isolate two values that drive your business, how might this diagram look to you?

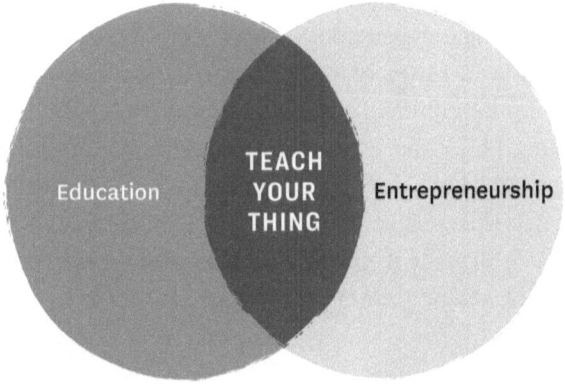

## A Method for Cultivating Warm Connections

To frame these conversations, I wrote a compelling question related to my unique mission: How can instructional design skills be leveraged to help purpose-driven small businesses thrive in today's niche economy? (For a refresher on unique mission, refer to the diagram on page 17.)

With my criteria in place, I made a list of people in four categories: friends, acquaintances, people doing aligned work, and thought leaders. I then reached out to them, one at a time, with a custom message about why I'd chosen them. Before asking if they'd meet for coffee, I referenced their work and shared why I admired them. I told them I was seeking out purpose-driven innovators to discuss leveraging education in business, an issue we both cared about. (My goal was to conduct thirty interviews, but in the end less than fifteen provided enough information to kick off my business.)

Gathering this feedback meant writing interview questions, taking detailed notes, and categorizing replies on a spreadsheet. I then identified patterns and built my services around common challenges these people faced.

Now, I offer the process as a jumping off point for you. Adapt it to your needs by using it to initiate informal one-on-ones with people you want to get to know over time. Or use it formally to check in with a group of your people before developing your next program.

Rather than thinking of networking as a chore, **let your community reveal opportunities everywhere you go.**

Cultivating warm connections is about intentional relationships, so it should feel light and invigorating, even if you're an introvert. Whether you meet in person or online is up to you. When you're ready, request conversations with people in the four categories that follow.

**Friends.** Begin by reaching out to friends. For me, this strategy ensured that I'd take action and not let fear get in the way. There's no shame in starting with familiar faces! In fact, I recommend it, especially if you've been hesitating or spinning your wheels. These can't be just any friends; they must be ones who need and want to solve the problem your business addresses. For me, one of those friends was Bethany Hegedus. She was a perfect choice. She's one of my ride-or-die pals who also runs a thriving business that features education programming. Though I knew the conversation would be compelling—it always is—this one surprised me by becoming transformational for us both. Unexpectedly, the topic of staff training came up. It helped her identify a new need for her growing business and helped me see a potential new offering for my services.

**Acquaintances.** Next, you're going to move on to acquaintances. For me, one was a colleague I'd worked with at the Minnesota History Center. Together we'd led one of my favorite projects, developing a multimedia activity kit for elementary and middle school students. I'd left the organization a few years earlier and hadn't thought about him in a while. But when I identified my criteria for these conversations, he came to mind instantly! He ran his own production studio on the side, and I knew he was committed to education and mission. So I reached out, and we had a coffee discussion that sparked my enthusiasm. He gave me several new things to consider for my business, including—wait for it—staff training.

**People doing aligned work.** Next, you're going to reach out to people doing work that's aligned with your unique mission. I leaned on an organization in the Twin Cities called Pollen Midwest. Knowing the importance of community, they host events where participants can opt in to sharing their contact information with fellow guests. I'd recently received a spreadsheet of 150 contacts from Pollen. After scouring the list and choosing five businesses that lit me up, I reached out: "Hey, we attended this Pollen event together. I'm developing new offerings for small businesses and I'm inspired by your commitment to education [based on an example specific to their work]. I'm a museum educator who's fascinated by the question of how learning design can help changemakers like you thrive in today's economy, which seems less stable but more open to purpose and creativity. I wonder if you'd meet with me to brainstorm ways my skills could help you as I start my own business." Reaching out like this felt vulnerable, but I believed enough in our shared values and goals to get past my fear. Ultimately, I met some amazing people through cultivating warm connections like this. Technically these people were strangers, but it never felt that way.

**Thought leaders.** Finally, you'll reach out to a thought leader, whether they're a podcaster you admire, an author, or somebody influential in your field.

I reached out to Deepa Iyer, author of *We Too Sing America: South Asian, Arab, Muslim, and Sikh Immigrants Shape Our Multiracial Future*, whom I discovered through a Medium article that inspired me deeply. She'd created an infographic about the social change ecosystem that had helped me own my worth as an educator and storyteller. I told her this when I reached out, and that I planned to use some of her teachings in my instruction. She later reached out to me and interviewed me as someone who had been affected by her work. During that Zoom call, we bonded over our overlapping missions. You never know what can happen if you take the risk and initiate a conversation! Just make sure that when you do, you ask how you can help them further their idea or promote their program. Then, follow through.

## The Power of Community

My story is just one example of what can happen when you tap into the wisdom of your community. Before these interviews, it had never occurred to me to offer coaching or content creation services related to staff training; they later became key offerings.

Too often when we think of amplifying a mission, we think we must shout it from the rooftops. Yes, that is one way to do it, but starting a dialogue doesn't have to be sexy. Even something as mundane as developing a service offering can present an opportunity to further your mission. It all comes down to finding the right people to jam with!

Cultivating warm connections is a habit that you can maintain in ways that make sense to you. Your people are already out there. They're already doing aligned work. Rather than thinking of networking as a chore, let your community reveal opportunities everywhere you go.

After I'd been doing this kind of community-building for a while, I was given an unexpected reminder of what a difference it can make. I'd just led a talk at a coworking space when an audience member approached me and said, "Isn't it so great that you could give this talk surrounded by friends?" Her comment surprised me because I'd known everyone in the room for less than a year, and some I'd only talked to once or twice. Upon reflection, I realized she was right—everyone here did feel like a friend. I'd worked hard to plan a meaningful event that would attract engaged participants, and because I was genuinely aligned with the attendees, the gathering was full of warmth. In the end, the coworking staff and I were pleased with how it turned out. The event even led to further connections, like a wellness leader who later interviewed me for his podcast.

Cultivating warm connections is rewarding, and your business is an ideal container in which to do it. But taking action as a purpose-driven leader can be scary. As you move forward, let me leave you with one of my favorite quotes. In her book *Playing Big*, Tara Mohr talks about two different kinds of fear. One can become debilitating, and it's the one we commonly think of when we're shaking in our boots. The other is called *yirah*, a Hebrew word whose meaning includes a sense of awe. As Mohr says in her book, "Awe has an element of fear in it—we humbly fear the greatness and grandness of what is before us—but awe encompasses so much more than fear."

As you start your own process for cultivating warm connections, may you experience *yirah*, finding reverence, appreciation, and inspiration. I can't wait to see what opens up for you along the way.

## ⓘ REFLECT

- What's a conversation you want to lead that's related to your big-hearted business?
- Name some warm connections who can help you get involved in an important, mission-driven dialogue.
- What do you think of Tara Mohr's description of the two types of fear (constrictive fear versus awe-based fear)?
- Name a time when you experienced fear based on being in the presence of greatness or awe.

## ☆ MAKE IT PRETTY

Write a compelling question related to your unique mission. Start by illustrating your own version of the diagram on page 17. Then, craft one open-ended question related to your people, problem, tasks, and income generation. Journal about how you can use this question to spark mutually beneficial conversations with warm people in your network.

## ♡ BRING IT TO LIFE

Brainstorm people you'd like to invite into a conversation about your big-hearted mission. List friends, acquaintances, people doing aligned work, and thought leaders.

# 14

# Shout from the Rooftops

EVERY CHANGEMAKER should be able to thrive wholeheartedly in their mission and get paid handsomely for it. And yet, too many common narratives say you can't succeed unless you run a certain type of business. "When people think of an entrepreneur in this current time, they typically imagine somebody who has some kind of tech or app idea that has the capacity to scale to every person in the world and can attract venture capital to do that," says Whitney Brimfield of Spark Point Fundraising. "When people say the bottom line is all that matters, that's patently untrue. I am an example of a mission-driven business and I know at least ten other people who are examples of it too."

This book is a call to all the big-hearted leaders to change the conversation and to amplify the belief that social entrepreneurship is a viable and fulfilling path. We can go about it in a variety of ways, and the remaining chapters cover specific tactics. My goal in sharing them isn't to imply you need to do them all; rather, consider them an invitation to act, to dig deep into your own true genius and use the ones that suit you best.

In this chapter, I'll cover two tools we can use to shout from the rooftops about the work we're doing: social media and newsletters. If shouting isn't your style, you can still use these tools to spark a conversation that's compelling, life-giving, and lovingly disruptive.

## Use Social Media... and Go All In

No matter what kind of product or service you offer, you have stories to tell. As business owners, we constantly hear about how we need to prioritize social media for this. If you're not yet regularly using social media, I'm not here to shame you for it (for all I know, you're already giving yourself a hard time for not doing enough). What I am here to do is help you learn from a purpose-driven business owner I admire who's fantastic at it and infuses every moment with joy.

Algernon Hall points out that social media is "a great tool to grow your business." But he also knows it's not just about putting yourself out there, it's about leading a meaningful dialogue.

Through videos of the assemblies his team puts on, he shows what learning should be: energized, collaborative, and fun. "Right now, in schools, there's a lot of negative energy, and many of these kids don't have a lot of examples to follow. I know because I was that kid. I have a gift for speaking, and I'm super creative. If I provide a little bit of positivity to offset that, I can help with the culture and the child."

Hall knows exactly who his people are and speaks directly to them. Though he's got way more to say than "buy my stuff," he's figured out how to sell effectively through social media. "I tag the schools I want to have partnerships with," he says. "So that counselor, that VP, that teacher, whoever's handling their Instagram account, they're going to look at what they were tagged in. And now that's bringing more eyes to the business."

By posting recaps of programs, Hall shows schools how he can adapt to meet their needs. "Principals are super, super busy. They may not have administrators in place, or some believe they can do everything in house, right? What I learned from a mentor is you post all assemblies. You post content when you leave, which keeps you in the face of educators and the public. As a principal, when you're winding down and scrolling through, you may have made a note to contact Algernon. But you didn't. So, this pops me back up at the top of your mind."

## Celebrate Your Clients and Community Members

Sharing about ourselves and our business doesn't come naturally to everyone. Several women business owners have told me being seen makes them feel so vulnerable that social media is terrifying. Facing this fear provides yet another opportunity to realize it's not about us. Done well, social

What values do you stand for, and what stories might you tell? **Possibilities are everywhere.**

media is about starting a dialogue. (Also, silence and powerlessness go hand in hand.) What debates in your field can you weigh in on? Who in your community deserves a shout-out?

Spark Point Fundraising addressed these questions through an ongoing social media campaign. It's called #BlackWomenSparkChange, and it highlights leaders in the nonprofit sector. The campaign celebrates clients and community members while furthering the company's values of ingenuity, equity, kindness, and a commitment to ending racism and amplifying nonprofits. Brimfield tells how the campaign came to be: "What I see, time and time again, is that when something bad is happening, people look to government. But it's just too much to expect of them. So, no matter what they don't do, somebody has to take up that slack. A lot of times, that's the nonprofit sector. But in a more local way, that's women—and in particular, women of color. They're the ones who are left with the greatest burdens because of the inequities of racism, white supremacy, and misogyny. All of that falls largely on Black women."

The campaign not only supports Spark Point's mission but also invites engagement. Followers can nominate individuals whose work should be elevated in the posts. Though technology often leads to disconnect, we can do things differently. Business leaders can and should prioritize connection, resilience, and humanity. As Brimfield points out, she wanted to avoid once again articulating what's wrong in our society, like systemic racism and violence against Black people.

Instead, she says, "I wanted Spark Point Fundraising to be part of amplifying what's good. If there were ever a time to recognize the incredible work of the nonprofit sector, it was [during the COVID-19 pandemic]. After all, nonprofit organizations were moving mountains to make sure that the most vulnerable people in our communities were protected and cared for."

In your own work, consider what a similar kind of amplification might look like. What values do you stand for and what stories might you tell? Possibilities are everywhere.

## Leverage a Newsletter for Direct Connection

I ran my business for nearly four years before establishing my newsletter and I regret not starting it sooner. When I think of the momentum I lost during that time, I kick myself for missing opportunities for growth. Though a newsletter may not sound sexy, I've found it to be the most reliable way to stay connected with my people. Though you may have heard others question whether newsletters are dead, they remain a highly effective way to gain traction. They provide something social media can't, which is direct access to your people and control over the experience.

One of my favorite parts of having a newsletter is the analytics. Social media analytics can be valuable too, but they have their limitations, such as a higher number of fake profiles and the fact that likes don't necessarily mean active engagement. With my newsletter, I always know whether people are reading or not and what content is resonating with them.

Though analytics can seem slightly creepy—I can see exactly who clicks on what—I'm in control of what to focus on. I don't see my subscribers as numbers; they're real people. If I could gather them in a living room, I would, but analytics will have to do as a stand in. They are clients I value deeply, community members I admire, and yes, even friends and family.

In the interest of honoring my subscribers' privacy (and protecting my own sanity), I have never once looked at who unsubscribes. I figure people have a right to shed a communication that no longer serves them, with no judgment from me. And I learned from my digital marketing strategist that people unsubscribing from your content can be a good thing because the goal is to reach people who *want* your content. It's better to have a smaller, engaged list than a deceptively high subscriber count. Inactive users bring your engagement numbers down, which isn't good for the health of your list. Even if you're not watching stats like open and click rates, email providers pay attention. Accounts with high unopen rates can (and should) be tagged as spammers.

If all this sounds overwhelming, keep in mind that hiring help is an option. Though it can be hard to let go of control at first, there are plenty of freelancers who are perfectly capable of capturing your voice or managing the details of operational data. After you've built a body of work in your newsletter, repurposing it elsewhere is a great way to maximize your work.

## Newsletters Don't Have to Be Fussy

As a writer and creative, I know newsletters don't have to be a chore, but I still saw them that way in the beginning. As it turned out, my readers responded most when I was having fun with my content. The year I launched my newsletter, my most-opened piece was called "My Experiment with Location Independence." It told the story of something I was shy to share at first: a 1,400-mile road trip my partner, Fred, and I took from Minnesota to New Mexico to work remotely for a month while spending time with family.

The piece was fun to write and it furthered a mission I care about: transforming our world of work to give people more agency over how they spend their time, talent, and energy.

Anne Ingersoll of College Bound Associates overcame her newsletter block after deciding not to write the piece she thought she "should" write on an expected topic in academic circles. Instead, she gave herself permission to write what was really on her mind. The holidays were coming, so she wrote a plea to families of high school students to stop bombarding them with questions about college around the dinner table. She urged them to get to know the high schoolers on a personal level instead. Concerned about the anxiety she sees in her clients, Ingersoll is committed to disrupting the status-driven ego of the college prep industry. Her newsletter was the perfect place for her to advocate for families to ignore expectations and help students find joy in the college search.

Dr. Abby Medcalf, a fun-loving author I know, wrote a book on romantic relationships called *Be Happily Married: Even If Your Partner Won't Do a Thing*. She calls her email campaigns "love letters" and infuses them with the humor her followers expect. I also chuckled when feminist author and speaker Geraldine DeRuiter, A.K.A. The Everywhereist, invited her Twitter fans to join her Super Cool Email Club.

After years of following her irreverent travel blog and social media posts, I happily signed up. I trusted her emails would take a stand for gender equality in the male-dominated restaurant world, all while making me laugh out loud.

In my case, setting up a newsletter was a bigger commitment than I thought it would be. But now that I have it, it's a reliable, fun way to engage with my people and spark dialogue about what really goes on in the life of a big-hearted strategist for education experiences.

> ### ❓ REFLECT
>
> - Of the people you follow on social media, who does the best job of amplifying their mission in a way that captures your attention?
> - Who in your community could use a shout-out on social media?
> - Who might you tag on social media when discussing a particular message?
> - What does another business do on social media that you'd like to replicate in your own way?
> - What's one way you could bring your unique mission to life in a newsletter?
> - List five questions you or others have about your unique mission. How could these be turned into an article or a series of posts?

- How do you (or how might you start to) use analytics to improve your business?

## ☆ MAKE IT PRETTY

Lists make great content for social media and newsletters. Come up with a topic related to your mission, then illustrate a journal entry about it. (Think, "Things I Wish I'd Known," "What If We Could Change the World," or "Old Rules That Must Go.")

## ♡ BRING IT TO LIFE

**Social Media.** Choose some hashtags that relate to your mission. Spend five minutes on your favorite platform exploring the conversations happening there.

**Newsletter.** Take five minutes to read a newsletter article from someone you respect. Consider what you liked about it and how you might replicate it.

# 15

# Build a Body of Work

A BEAUTIFUL THING about big-hearted entrepreneurs is the energy we throw into our offerings—but sometimes our relational enthusiasm keeps us from developing our own body of work. I've seen it in my peers and experienced it myself: The problem we see in the world continues to gnaw at us. We yearn to take a more active role in addressing it, but everyday roadblocks get in the way. Urgent projects take the lead while we hesitate to take the next step. Sooner or later, the time comes when the pain of holding back our deeper message is no longer okay. Our dissatisfaction grows, gaining force gradually until it outweighs the pull of our everyday hesitations.

Do you want to step back from your business agenda, clarify your area of expertise, and lead transformational discourse? In this chapter, I'll cover two more ways to go about it: blogging and podcasting. Only you know which format suits your style, but especially if longer conversation is your thing, one or both methods may be up your alley.

Barb Buckner Suárez runs a successful practice and develops an impressive array of content, including a newsletter, blog, social media presence, and podcast. Each format furthers her mission of transforming how we talk about parenting, drives her business, and opens doors to new places to share her countercultural message.

But that's not how things started out. Buckner Suárez didn't get into the groove of creating content until *after* she'd spent a year beating herself up for not writing the book she'd been dreaming of. During a heart-to-heart with a mentor, she admitted she was super frustrated with herself. Fortunately, she says, "He did not laugh at me, which I've always appreciated. He encouraged me to go home and write a blog. 'You'll be able to hit publish over and over again,' he said."

"The idea of all these little mini pieces appealed to me. And because it's me—go big or go home—I started the 31 Day Project. I did a blog post every day for the month of October. I came home and I just did it, right? I didn't get stuck or locked into perfectionism." Buckner Suárez finally found herself building a body of work, one blog post at a time.

## Build a Body of Work, One Blog Post at a Time

Chronic busyness keeps you reactive. It prevents you from furthering your mission, so you need to make space for writing—more accurately, you need to make space to think.

When you make time to think and write, you begin to bolster your ideas, gaining clarity on exactly what your unique contribution can and should be. Consider this quote from the late journalist Joan Didion's piece "Why I Write": "Had I been blessed with even limited access to my own mind there would have been no reason to write. I write entirely to find out what I'm thinking, what I'm looking at, what I see and what it means. What I want and what I fear."

In my case, blogging preceded business ownership. Years before launching Teach Your Thing, in my phase of growing employee frustration, I started a blog to remind myself I had a voice. I began to rely on it to sort out my thoughts, and it increased my confidence in my mission as a result. This led to finding more collaborators who revealed new possibilities, provided a sense of community, and strengthened my resolve to keep fighting for what matters.

### Activate Your Voice through Podcasting

When I interviewed Buckner Suárez, she'd just completed the third season of her podcast *Birth Happens*, which repurposes her other writing. To an outside observer, hearing how polished and well-crafted it sounds, it may seem like its creation came easily. But developing the podcast's format required her to own her creative process and not let other voices dampen her vision. "It was really important to me that it provide exactly what I was hoping for," she says. "So, it took a long time. At least initially, I was not interested in an interview model. That felt a little too close to 'calling in the experts.'" Along with featuring her signature relatability, the podcast allows Buckner Suárez to speak directly about her core values. The theme of each season captures a different value, including intimacy, vulnerability, and connection.

"My husband Roberto is an amateur podcaster and he's the producer. He's the one who makes it sound so good. But in the beginning, he said, 'Hey, I found this bit of music.' And I'm like, 'Nope, that's not it.' He went, 'Oh, wow, you feel very strong about that,' and I said, 'I have a vision. I know exactly how I want it to sound.'"

Now that the duo has eighteen episodes under their belt, they've developed the structure that meets her vision of compelling storytelling that provides comfort to a parent who wants to hear from someone who feels like a cool aunt.

Now, when Buckner Suárez considers what's next, she has a body of work to point to. Having established her message through her first three seasons, she's built a foundation to expand on. She's finally ready to amplify her mission in a new way by bringing others into the dialogue. "Now, I'm finding myself saying, 'I could talk with that person,' or 'That person and I align really well; we could have a conversation about this.'"

Once big-hearted entrepreneurs are thriving in their element, they are well-positioned to collaborate with fellow aligned leaders. One of Buckner Suárez's goals is to amplify Black voices in the world of birth, and future seasons may be where she does that. "We know about inequities in morbidity rates and I'm here to try my best to close that gap. How can I amplify folks that are actually doing the work in this world?" she wonders. "That really appeals to me. So having a whole season, that would be just fabulous."

Your unique point of view emerges over time **as you refine your thoughts.**

## Five Strategies for Building Your Body of Work

Crafting a body of work is a journey. No matter what medium you choose, you need to create, over and over again. You must speak regularly enough for your ideas to build on each other. Let them evolve. Your unique point of view emerges over time as you refine your thoughts. To establish your content creation habit, use these strategies to set yourself up for success.

**Strategy one: Explore what you want.** Joy is way more important than perfection, especially if you're new to the habit of creating. Give yourself permission to say what you want, not what you think you should say. Far too many of us believe doing what we want makes us selfish. Tapping into your unique genius can be healing and inherently joyful. Create for the people who light you up. The sooner you stop worrying about whether you're good enough, the sooner you can start creating. Resist the pressure to talk like you have it all figured out and write to the people you'd invite for coffee—or in my case, tea. As a frequent reader of books on purpose-driven business, I have no patience for "expert" authors who talk down to me or feel the need to prove how accomplished they are. Speak as the compassionate human you are, the one who can show your followers you've been where they are now.

**Strategy two: Let curiosity take the lead.** What would happen if you saw content creation as thinking time? Give yourself the gift of finding out what's in your head. Interview someone who inspires you, offer tips on something you've learned, tell a story about your everyday work, research topics your people are jamming about, share an unpopular opinion, or explore wisdom from outside your niche. There are infinite ways to go about it, so follow your bliss. My first blog was a place to share my sewing projects. Over time, I realized what made me curious was the act of creation and self-discovery. In time, this led to my next blog, *Resounding You*, which eventually led me to launch a business.

**Strategy three: Extend your time frame for accomplishment.** You can't build a body of work without consistency. Especially in the early days, stop beating yourself up for how little you've accomplished. Your ideas need time to blossom. Take the amount of time you think it'll take to develop a body of work that impresses you and double it. Brilliance, and sometimes even coherent thought, comes from consistency. Designate a spot on your calendar for blogging or podcasting, then block it indefinitely. Sure, you may struggle to use this time at first, but keep it on the calendar. Find a physical space where you can focus without distraction and make it your happy place. Then, keep showing up.

**Strategy four: Share your content with real people.** Creating isn't enough to start a dialogue. You need to proactively share your work. My blogs grew a following when I adopted the practice of telling people what I'd written—I mean *actual* people, people I'd met and knew by name (gasp). That said, sharing my posts didn't mean I spammed my friends and family, or anyone for that matter. When sharing your work with others, ask yourself: How can my content cultivate warm connections?

**Strategy five: Put your antenna up for people who already care about the topics you're exploring.** When a mutual topic of interest comes up organically, let people know you've written about it. (Maybe you wrote the post months ago, but it's relevant now. Send it their way!) Also, find engaged communities to converse with. Many forums allow members to share their work, so follow their guidelines and go for it. One community I joined has a daily thread where you can post, but only if you read and comment on three other posts. This is a great model to follow. Every time I post there or elsewhere, I comment on at least three other people's stuff. Remember, it's not about putting yourself out there, it's about starting a dialogue.

## Five Strategies for Building Your Body of Work

1. Explore what you want (not what you think you should want).
2. Let curiosity take the lead.
3. Extend your time frame for accomplishment.
4. Share your content with real people.
5. Put your antenna up for those who already care about the topics you're exploring.

## ⓘ REFLECT

- Name three things you truly want to write about, so much so that the thought lights you up.
- What's getting in the way of your writing?
- What's your favorite blog or podcast and why?
- How will you demonstrate your core values through your blog or podcast?
- Do you have a body of work? Can you repurpose it in new ways?

## ☆ MAKE IT PRETTY

To generate topic ideas, do a mind map. Start with a big idea, then brainstorm smaller topics that relate to it. Make your mind map look like bubbles. Set a timer for seven minutes and see how many topics you can generate. Include your core values, questions your audience cares about, and anything that lights you up about the topic, then go back and review your topics. What categories do they fall into? Choose a color for each and color the bubbles accordingly.

## ♡ BRING IT TO LIFE

Research three online communities whose conversations inspire you. Find out their rules for posting work. Visit them three days a week for five minutes, commenting actively. Any time you create a blog post or podcast episode, post it there.

# 16

# Get Your Event On

Hosting an event is a great way to break through the isolation of our world and get people talking. If you enjoy bringing folks together, consider whether this might help you advance your mission organically, without feeling forced. Think about the people in your community who already care about the problem your business addresses. If you were to gather them to share ideas, what might it look like? (Let yourself dream!)

One of the most impactful things I've done since becoming an entrepreneur is to jointly host an event called Life Pie: An Evening of Women's Storytelling. Two friends and I ran it together, and its effects rippled through my life and work for months afterward. As my cohosts Kate Stower and Jenia Strom discovered, hosting an event also provides an ideal opportunity to tap into the wisdom of your community.

We built Life Pie out of a desire to empower women. We'd been meeting weekly in an informal writing group that Stower had established. Over coffee and journaling, we realized that two of us had stories we yearned to tell, but there weren't a lot of forums in which to tell them. We also had the chops to build a forum ourselves (all of us had developed programs in the past), so we decided to go for it.

## Solve a Problem in Community

Solving a problem for yourself can open doors for others. Stower describes our motivation this way: "Women have such collective wisdom and such a variety of different life experiences. Sometimes we are hesitant to tell those stories, especially in front of a wider audience. So, it felt like a natural fit for us to host a program." Soon, our writing group turned into a planning group.

We knew we wanted a variety of stories—funny and serious—told by women of different ages and backgrounds. To recruit storytellers, we brainstormed possible categories, which Stower drew in her notebook as slices in a pie. Now, we had our structure. We hoped to gather at least one storyteller for each of the following topics:

- Relationships and belonging
- Creativity and play
- Wellness and spirituality
- Career and work
- Learning and growth
- Money and freedom

Soon after, a mission-driven leader who shared our enthusiasm, Kelly Pratt, offered up the perfect venue. Pratt lives in a St. Paul artist loft complex with an event space, and she runs an online community of heart-centered and soul-led women called Athena Village. (Talk about aligned values!) As it happens, she'd just developed categories for her own programming that overlapped our list so closely it was almost spooky.

## Recruit Collaborators Who'll Help Your Mission Shine

Next, we brainstormed who might make a good emcee, someone with the personality to carry a room. A former colleague of Stower's and mine came to mind instantly; we had both relished working with her at the Minnesota History Center. Her name is Wendy Freshman, coauthor of *Making History: Have a Blast with 15 Crafts*, and we were delighted when she agreed. Like us, she had experience running events and developing curricular materials. Over the years, we'd collaborated with fellow team members and community partners to create a variety of public programs and teacher workshops that I still think were epic.

By now, even though our event was in the early stages, we'd managed to pull together a dream team. We had plenty of ideas, but a successful event only has as much time as your audience will allow. "We knew a lot of moms would be giving up bedtime routines at home with kids, and a lot of women would be coming after work. We could not host a five-hour event," Stower explains. Our vision included a social hour afterward, where we'd serve pie. We wanted the

Whatever goal you wish to achieve for your mission, **you'll serve it better by creating space for people to engage.**

audience to meet the storytellers, informally sharing stories of their own.

Our original thought was to recruit ten speakers. But we needed to keep the storytelling to about an hour, so we ended up with fewer speakers and we allotted them seven minutes each. As a mission-driven leader, it can be easy to get caught up in all your great ideas. Though you have an exciting message to share, your event is about your audience, not you. When in doubt, shorten your content.

## Make Space for Attendees to Engage

When conceiving of your own program, think of ways to involve your audience from the outset.

One of the worst things you can do is rush your audience. Whatever goal you wish to achieve, you'll serve it better by creating space. Yes, your content matters, but it's never more important than letting your participants engage. You must be ruthless about distilling the number of things you expect to happen at any given event.

When all was said and done, our event hit our goal of one hundred attendees. (Along with being our venue's limit, that size turned out to be just right for the energy we hoped to generate.) Though Stower and I spoke at the event, we both knew our stories were only part of the experience. As she points out, "You can only control the message you're delivering. You can't control what the audience is hearing. With all those people coming from different walks of life, you really have to vary the program as much as you can."

In our case, that meant making use of the venue's community space. It has two rooms, which is ideal for allowing participants to get up and move during the second half of the evening. We set chairs in one room for storytelling and displayed pies in the other, with several stations for gathering in small groups.

## Match the Bandwidth of Your People

Let's consider another example of an event you could host: a workshop.

Liz Dempsey Lee offers an intriguing example. To further her mission of bringing more equity to schools, families, and communities, Dempsey Lee leads programs designed to foster meaningful conversations, like Beyond the Yard Sign: Being Equitable in Everyday Life.

Recognizing that our collective bandwidth was noticeably low after pandemic isolation, she created an event format called Not a Book Club. She loves the level of engagement it brings, so she's offered it in various settings, including for parent groups and nonprofit leaders.

Here's how it works. For five weeks, one evening a week, participants gather for a ninety-minute video conversation. Grounding the discussion is a series of resources Dempsey Lee has provided the group. "People want to learn more about these topics, like racial equity or intersectionality, but books about them tend to be really academic and very thick. I'm deeply interested and even I fall asleep reading them sometimes."

She created five short readings or videos on topics such as "What is intersectionality?" and "How does parenting interact with racial discrimination?" Attendees commit to reading or watching at least one per week, or more if they choose. "The idea is to create a safe space to allow questions to be asked and to give some sort of basic information. It's a way to get everybody with the same base of information in a way that doesn't knock them out."

I admire Dempsey Lee's program for a variety of reasons. For one, it demonstrates solid instruction design principles, like keeping things simple and giving participants choice. But what I find even more compelling is that she's used her unique skills to address an important problem and generate income. She's found a way to own her worth, bringing together her PhD-level training and her ability to disrupt a problem in society that breaks her heart.

## Incorporate Mission and Flow

Event producer Matthew Cibellis of Cibellis Solutions reinforces the notion that careful event design leads to better outcomes for your mission. "You have to incorporate two things: mission and flow. Without these, it's like someone's talking at you for thirty minutes about why their organization is the most important thing ever, right? It becomes preachy, even though you're in front of a choir who's on board with you."

Cibellis acknowledges that it can be easy, even for experienced instructors, to fall into the trap of trying to cover too many things during an event. I too have seen this time and time again with my clients, and I'd be lying if I said I hadn't overstuffed a program or two myself. As mission-driven folks, we get so enthusiastic about our mission that we forget not everyone lives and breathes the same ideas we do.

So, if you're someone who's dying to run an event but never finds the time, consider making time for one this year. What if you simplified your idea? And what if you didn't have to do it all alone?

## ⓘ REFLECT

- What event would you like to host in the short-term? In the long-term?

- How might an event further your unique mission?

- What if you let go of the idea that your event must be chock-full of information you generate yourself? How might you curate content from others?

- How might you tap into your community's wisdom to plan or run this event? Who might you collaborate with?

- How will you make time for planning your online or in-person event?

## ☆ MAKE IT PRETTY

Fill an entire page with a wash of watercolor paint. Then, capture in words or images details about a favorite event you attended, socially or for business. How did you feel when you were there? How did the organizers let you know you were welcome upon arrival? How did they set the flow? What was the energy like? How did connection with others happen? Write about how you might structure your own event to replicate this feeling.

## ♡ BRING IT TO LIFE

If you were to host an event, where would it take place? Research venues in your area. How much do they cost? How might the venues themselves provide an opportunity to attract the right audience? What is the vibe of the space? How could you use it to create flow?

# Develop a Signature Talk

IN THIS chapter, we'll explore another vital tool for getting your message out: giving a signature talk. In this case, I'm referring to a presentation that any purpose-driven business owner can use to attract the right people to their consultancy or program. (It's a different ball game for keynoters who make a living through their stage gigs, and that's not my focus here.)

The length of your signature talk can vary based on your audience's needs and can be anything from, say, a ten-minute introduction to a ninety-minute workshop. A signature talk can be equally dynamic in person or online; neither is inherently good or bad—though if you do choose both, as I do, you'll need to adapt how you facilitate it. It may or may not feature slides (my talks always have them—oddly enough, designing slide decks is one of my favorite tasks! But I beg of you, if you do include slides, please, please avoid the "death by too much text" trap).

What makes a talk your signature is that it captures your uniqueness and shows people the problem you solve, why it matters to you, and whether you're the right person for them. Finally, signature talks can be delivered as paid workshops or as unpaid experiences. I've done both, depending on my goals. Now, let's investigate what it takes to ensure your talk is powerful, relevant, and engaging.

## Make Your Message Relatable

Barb Buckner Suárez's work is based on neuroscience, but she's determined to make it relatable. Months before I interviewed her, she'd given a talk on the maternal brain at a conference filled with academics, practitioners, and therapists. "My presentation is one long story," she says. "Yeah, there's a premise and there's research that backs it up, but it comes back around to a story." After the talk, a therapist approached her and said, "That is the first time I've actually heard someone talk about the brain without making me feel stupid." This moment was not only fulfilling for Buckner Suárez but also proof that she's furthering her mission. "Why would you craft a message that's not understandable or relatable?" she wonders. "You could talk as much as you want, but it's not going to make any difference, right?"

Whether or not you call yourself one, you too are likely a subject matter expert. You may have spent years, even decades, improving your craft, refining your methodology, and working with your audience. In a world that says we must prove ourselves constantly, it can be easy to think giving talks is about imparting our wisdom. Of course you have knowledge to share, but a talk isn't about you or your content—it's about empowering your people to improve their lives by doing things differently.

## More Than One?

I started developing my own signature talks about three years into my business, when one-on-one networking became overwhelming. Note that, yes, I just said "talks," plural. This leads to an inevitable question: Can I have more than one signature talk? You'll get different answers depending on who you ask, but I've embraced the idea that more than one is okay. The bigger problem is not having one at all.

Before I go on, let me include a disclaimer. I've heard speakers argue that to generate income and find clients, one signature talk is all you need. I concede their point that continually creating new talks sucks up your time and dilutes your message. Moving the needle—for ourselves, our business, and society—depends on *focused* momentum. Sending too many messages confuses people. If you decide to develop more than one signature talk, you still need to limit them to what you want to be known for.

We as founders must do what works for us. Each of us is at a different place in our business journey, but we must start somewhere. Visionaries solving massive societal problems may need to give a few talks to figure out exactly what their signature content should be. Refining your messaging

**Your signature talk captures your uniqueness and shows people the problem you solve,** why it matters to you, and whether you're the right person for them.

requires distilling, then distilling again (and for most of us, again and again). This is true even if your medium is writing, podcasting, or social media. Saying our ideas out loud to a group is one of the fastest ways to figure out what stays and what should go.

## Test Out Ideas

If you're an introvert or highly sensitive (I happen to be both), developing a signature talk allows you to think through what you want to say before you say it. You can also engage communities to test out which ideas related to your mission have traction.

I developed my first round of signature talks for an organization called SCORE, the largest network of volunteer business mentors in the US. The Twin Cities host a thriving chapter that offers three workshops a week. After using a SCORE mentor myself, I wanted to help others and pitched my services as a presenter.

I'd spent my first few years in business customizing my learning strategy services and was committed to narrowing my focus. I had a bunch of ideas for talks, so I emailed their workshop coordinator with a list of options. (Note that to get this far, I'd already filtered them by subjects that aligned with my unique mission.) These topics met my criteria for being worth my time: they discuss a societal problem that breaks my heart, make use of skills that light me up, and cover a service people are willing to pay for. Now, I needed to complete the picture by hearing what resonated with my people.

Before long, I heard back. Their small committee had chosen their top three. Boom! They'd eliminated a few topic ideas, which showed me exactly what to focus on. Had I not solicited feedback, I may have wasted time stewing over less valuable content; worse yet, I may have squandered weeks developing it. Now, armed with data, I put dates on the calendar. The three workshops occurred over several months, giving me space to develop one talk at a time.

## Benefit Your Business, Amplify Your Mission

Those talks went so well that SCORE booked me to deliver them again throughout the year. The following year, we repeated the cadence. Did any of those topics become my one-and-only, the signature message I'd be known for forever? No. But developing and delivering them did allow me to refine my content, see opportunities for growth, and gain a new burst of energy. Here are some benefits you might seek when building your own.

**Build trust.** A signature talk builds trust. It lets people get to know you in a nonthreatening setting. Once they've learned something from you, they're considerably more likely to engage with you, advocate for your business, and hire you.

**Book clients.** If you don't like chasing clients but thrive on helping people, consider building your business by giving a signature talk. When I deliver workshops to SCORE, the number of registrants averages between sixty and seventy-five. Some talks are in person and some are online, but a quarter to half of the registrants usually show up. (This is higher than average for free seminars, which speaks to the organization's strong reputation in the Twin Cities' small-business community.)

I can recoup the cost of planning and delivering a talk if I book just one client as a result. For repeats of a topic I've already developed, my return on investment goes up even more. Not every talk generates leads, but these talks have generated some of my favorite clients. Attendees have signed up for my cohort program and become superstar contributors, booked me for one-on-one learning strategy coaching, and in one case, referred me to a cultural center that hired me for a substantial project developing a fascinating series of school activities.

**Grow your list.** There's no way around it. If you want your business to grow, you need to find ways to increase your list of potential clients. As my digital marketing specialist once told me, "New people are the lifeblood of your business."

I stand firmly against pushy sales tactics. I have never, and won't ever, engage in them. Giving talks is a great alternative to attract the right people to your business. Your promo copy should capture the values your brand stands for, and your talking points should do the same. For example, my slides reference social entrepreneurship throughout, allowing my audience to self-select who wants to hear more from me.

As a bonus, SCORE provides speakers with a list of the names and emails of all registrants. I treat this list with care and don't abuse the privilege of receiving it, but I do send a few follow-up emails giving people content refreshers and the chance to engage further with Teach Your Thing.

**Increase visibility.** Giving talks is a great way to increase your visibility. Even though I love to get on my soapbox and complain about the phrase "put yourself out there," business growth depends on making yourself seen. Visibility often brings credibility. In a world that tells social entrepreneurs their goals are foolish, giving talks allows you to share the good work that's actually happening. Your unique point of view is beneficial to others, so don't be shy about sharing it. If you want to disrupt a tired status quo in your profession or community, don't discount this tool for shining a light on the people, solutions, and messages that should be out in the open.

**Build confidence.** Sure, it's a common narrative that the average person is terrified of public speaking. And many of us do fear being seen, especially when standing up for something meaningful to us. As an introvert who has overcome these fears herself, I can tell you that sharing your message with real people can also be a great way to *build* confidence.

By inviting people into a compelling conversation, you attract others who care about it too. Often, I find it comforting to meet these folks and hear from them. Responding to questions and observing what resonates with your people also helps you strengthen your message. The more you talk in front of a group, the easier it gets. And remember, venues come in many shapes and sizes, so you get to decide which ones work for you.

**Promote dialogue.** Giving a talk is a chance to listen. If you want to make a difference, you need to stay in regular dialogue with your audience. I recommend building time for audience interaction into every talk. There's a saying I learned in my stint as a corporate Learning Design Strategist: "The person doing the talking is the person doing the learning."

As amazing as your content is, resist the urge to fill the whole space with your voice. Every interaction you facilitate gives you information about your audience, including what they need, what they doubt, and what they desire. Pay attention. This data is critical for ensuring your offerings continue to serve them effectively.

Follow-up conversations are part of the fun too! You get to meet aligned humans who care about similar things. As every business owner should know, high-value leads matter. Most talks I give spark further conversation, often leading to discovery calls with individuals who are well informed about my services, and thus likelier to purchase them.

## ? REFLECT

- What topics could you talk about repeatedly?
- Do you need more than one signature talk right now? Why or why not?
- How might giving a talk be a viable way for you to generate high-quality leads?
- Can you see yourself giving your talk in person, online, or both?
- How many clients or leads would you need to attract from a given talk to make it worthwhile?

## ☆ MAKE IT PRETTY

Consider the visuals for your talk. If you'll be using a slide deck, there are no excuses for boring, text-heavy slides. Today's software allows you to create vibrant, clean visuals that encourage comprehension and engagement. Research tools for designing slides. Play around to get to know them. There are so many tricks you can use.

## ♡ BRING IT TO LIFE

Research three to ten groups who might want to hear a talk about your mission. Brainstorm industry conferences, association events, corporate teams, nonprofits, chambers of commerce, special interest groups, universities, schools, and community organizations. Find out who the venue's contact is and reach out.

# Teach Your Thing

TEACHING WHAT you know can be one of the most direct ways to amplify your business's unique mission. It also feels good. Every time Mindy Martell of Clothier Design Source leads a session for her online program, The Apparel Mentor, she "feels 100 percent jazzed. It's a shot of inspiration every time. It's what I love to do." For Martell, turning her methods into a learning experience is a win-win: aspiring designers gain the knowledge to get factories to take them seriously, and she benefits from an additional, dependable income stream. Her live monthly mentorship program builds a strong sense of community, reinforces her industry authority, and provides a non-pushy opportunity for marketing services at her design house and factory. But it's not just about the bottom line; it never has been. Disrupting unjust labor practices was a motivator for starting her factory in the first place, and now teaching allows her to show others their power to revolutionize the fashion industry through ethical manufacturing.

My other clients also blow me away with their subject matter expertise. Most of them are what I'd call naturals at teaching, but when they develop their own course or workshop, they know too much. Making an impact requires distilling information for your people's needs, and it's easy to get lost in that information. A thought may have crossed your mind: "Just because I know and love my thing doesn't mean I know how to teach it, Suzi." I understand. In this chapter, I'll cover a few solutions that accompany my work and can be straightforward to apply, even if you don't know anything about instructional design.

## Flip Your Learning Environment

If you've ever taken an online course on demand, you intuitively understand the concept of a flipped classroom. (Educators use this term to refer to a kind of learning experience that technology has made popular.) In a flipped classroom, the learner encounters the content at home and works through it during class, rather than being introduced to the content in a class and studying it at home. This approach assumes direct instruction is not the best use of class time, and I agree! Think about it. When you're learning something new, would you rather use time with your instructor to ask personalized questions, or sit silently while they lecture at you?

When I met Martell, she was revamping the lessons that now make up the Apparel Mentor. Years before, she had established the program as an in-person workshop. Apparel entrepreneurs from outside St. Paul had to invest in travel to Martell's factory if they wanted to learn from her.

Through our work together, Martell rethought how she delivered her lessons and moved much of her content online. As she did, she flipped her lessons, transforming the Apparel Mentor experience. It not only saved her and her staff time but also maximized engagement for participants who access the content by joining her membership community. Now, students can watch and rewatch her lessons any time, from the comfort of their homes or the convenience of their phones. For live mentorship, she offers office hours at select times. Rather than hearing a lecture during precious time with Martell and her staff, community members use weekly group time to ask questions about challenges they're facing.

## Provide a Community Component

Course creators often get hung up on presenting their content perfectly. However, I'd argue that you should spend just as much time, if not more, creating a meaningful experience. I'll let you in on a secret: your content matters, but it's not what transforms things. It's not what inspires behavior change, and it may not even be why people sign up for your program. If you build a supportive culture into your course, participants are far likelier to experience breakthroughs simply by supporting one another.

People won't automatically know what's expected of them in your space, so it's up to you to develop guidelines and tell them. For example, will your program include an online forum? When people first sign up, make it clear what kind of participation is expected and what's unacceptable, then prompt them along the way. Say your group celebrates wins on Wednesdays. Send a reminder email each week with ideas about how to share these wins. When someone posts, be sure to respond! If you've ever posted in a community and been met with silence, you know how unwelcoming it can be. After that, did you stick around?

As Martell can confirm, a community can turn participants into rabid fans. "When people start their journey as apparel entrepreneurs, they feel they're the only people who are stupid and don't get it. Then, once they join the community, they realize no, that's just how it is. It's a confusing industry and nobody gets it. And they're also not feeling alone anymore. They're cheering each other on. They're lifting each other up. They're asking questions the others might not have thought of, and they're learning from each other just by bringing up different topics."

We live in a world of crushing isolation. Creating a learning experience that shows your people they're not alone will inspire their deep appreciation. If your program helps them make the changes they've been yearning for, they'll become your biggest advocates.

## Tell Stories

When creating a course, one of the most impactful things you can do is tell stories—including your own. In Martell's case, stories are directly tied to amplifying her mission. "I generally share stories about what it's like traveling overseas and visiting other factories. One client was going to make [their clothing] overseas, and after I shared the horrible stories of things I've experienced there and seen, they pivoted. They decided to raise their price points and go after a slightly different target market, and they're manufacturing in the US right now. That's huge."

When designing your course, chances are good you'll be tempted to overload your people with too much information. Take a page from Martell's playbook and make space to tell your story too!

## Be a Guide on the Side

Again, effective teaching isn't about content, it's about behavior change. There's a saying my teacher colleagues and I used during my museum days: "Don't be a sage on the stage, be a guide on the side." The K–12 teachers we supported were familiar with this phrase, as well as the understanding that their role isn't to spoon-feed content through lectures and presentations. Rather, their job is to facilitate experiences that lead students to discover the learning on their own.

This philosophy is still a cornerstone of my work. I find it endlessly valuable for my clients, who can feel pressure from their industry to prove themselves constantly. Jason Jones of The Coaching Hour puts it beautifully: "I have found that most people [who take my program Adaptive Conversations for Conscious Sales] can do most everything. They don't need to be taught. They need to experience it enough to recognize they can already do it. They need to be hungry enough to want to change and actually start doing it. It's not about knowing, it's about experiencing."

When people struggle to make the changes they seek, they often know what to do, yet some other barrier is in the way. As you develop your own learning experience, pay attention. What might your audience's roadblocks be: A deeply held belief that change isn't possible? Lack of support from their loved ones? A related habit that throws them off track? Something in their physical environment? In your instruction, name these barriers out loud and support your people as they remove them themselves.

## Provide Structure

Another factor that's critically important is providing consistent instruction. Take Jones's business, for example. When I worked with him, he was preparing for exponential growth. For him, that meant developing a training program that could be delivered reliably, no matter who would be teaching his work in the future.

"My business has quickly moved from [just me] training people to bringing in more trainers, or companies to train their people. It's moving into where I'll be training and certifying trainers who will be delivering the programs they license from me." Jones and I did several things to make the experience repeatable. Primary among them was writing a script to accompany the training deck, rather than relying on the presenter to speak extemporaneously. We also

If you build a supportive culture into your course, participants will experience breakthroughs **simply by supporting one another.**

ensured the design elements—like section headers, learning objectives, and discussion prompts—were consistent in terms of scope and visual design.

Consistency for scaling was important for Spark Point Fundraising as well. Although we created a very different product (a staff operations manual), the goal was the same: scaling operations for a quickly growing company. As founder Whitney Brimfield puts it, "You can't really scale a professional services business without some sort of structure that enables people to replicate things."

She describes why investing in training was worth it: "If you're in a period of significant growth, the way you've done things is the biggest part of your value as a company. It not only helps you grow but also enables somebody else to come along and run the company just the way you did, without a lot of effort."

Brimfield has always tracked her operations. When we worked together, it was clear from her staff's devotion to her that she'd long taken the time to share with them not just her "hows" but also her "whys." "I have the sense that most entrepreneurs, on some level, are extreme control freaks," she admits. "If you're trying to scale an enterprise, and you've had control over every single aspect in detail for so long, you need to cede control to other people to grow. There are very few comfortable ways to do that. The best one I found is to write down everything exactly the way I want it to be."

Despite Brimfield's self-described desire for control, she values her team's opinions and ideas for improving the company's workflow and client interactions. When I helped develop their manual, she made sure I interviewed everyone—from leadership to interns—to glean their insights about the operational categories we catalogued, such as marketing, finance, and client onboarding.

There are a variety of ways you can teach your thing, from workshops to courses to staff training. Whether your company is growing, or your business model relies on providing empowering programs, I trust you'll find that developing learning experiences is an effective way to increase your impact and amplify your mission.

> ## ⑦ REFLECT
>
> - Does teaching light you up? Why or why not?
> - What topics are you uniquely suited to teach as a class, workshop, or course?
> - What stories can you tell during your training that might motivate your people and engender their trust in you?
> - What behaviors do your learners need to change?
> - How can your learning experience remove barriers to changing those behaviors?
> - How might you design a community component?
> - How can you bring consistency to the experience each time the class is taught?

## ☆ MAKE IT PRETTY

Think of a learning experience you might want to create and draw it as a flipped classroom. Show how the students access the content, depict where they gather, and illustrate how they support each other.

## ♡ BRING IT TO LIFE

To prepare to design your own learning experience, research ones that already exist. List their pros and cons. Do you like the length of the class? Does it have a community component? What do you think of the look and feel? What vibe does the facilitator bring to the experience? List ways your own experience would improve on theirs or represent your own unique medicine.

# 19

# Propel Your People

IN PART one, we explored ways to own your worth. Treating your time, talent, energy, and money with love is fundamental to any big-hearted entrepreneurship journey. So far in part two, we've explored ways to amplify your mission. As we wrap this part up, I'd like to reinforce the reason you do all this in the first place: to propel your people to live better lives. Here are some strategies for arranging and presenting your ideas in a way that sparks them into action.

## Give Them a Hook

When I was a museum educator, one of my favorite historians, Annette Atkins, taught me a wise lesson about creating irresistible learning experiences: "Grab their attention in the first thirty seconds, or you may lose them forever." My colleagues and I hired her multiple times over the years to lead workshops for our teachers. She was not only deeply respected for her scholarship and writing but also legendary for wowing every audience. One of her hallmarks was to build a story around an everyday object. She wove in layers of history to show, not just tell, the significance of an era or a moment. In my favorite of her workshops, she began by asking participants to take off one shoe and put it in the middle of a table. She then told stories about the cultural significance of shoes throughout the decades.

Later, when I worked with my client Cindy Karnes, founder of the Empowered Hours Club, we developed two talks to motivate her community of ambitious entrepreneurs. The first covered her bread and butter at the time, social media strategy, and the second expanded her offerings by highlighting her newest content: action plans for accomplishing epic dreams.

In both cases, Karnes speaks directly to her audience's deepest concerns while showing what she solves for them and how. Her broader talk, Creating Unstoppable Momentum, kicks off with a question: "This year, how many of you set a big, hairy goal for your business or life?" She asks for volunteers to share who has achieved one of their goals and who's still working on one. Right away, Karnes captures her audience's attention. She gets them to imagine where they want to go, which sets up the strategies for mindset, planning, and implementation that she's about to cover.

Her original talk, "Social Media Strategy: Increasing Visibility with Intention," hooks attendees with a slide featuring three pained emojis. She asks, "How many of you feel this way when you think about social media for your business?" Then, her second slide shows three joyful emojis. Karnes shows her people right away that she's here to address their pain points and show what's possible. Social media can be impactful, profitable, and fun—just ask her.

## Identify Your Learning Objectives

A transformative learning experience isn't about imparting knowledge, it's about empowering your people to do something differently in their life or work. Ask yourself, "What do I intend for people to *do* after encountering this program?" Too many of us start the planning process by vomiting out every thought in our heads. Instead, put your audience first. Zero in on what behaviors could change their lives. The goals you identify will become your learning objectives. Note that a learning objective doesn't have to be dramatic—it could be simply seeing something in a new way—but it does have to be actionable.

In the case of Karnes's social media talk, one learning objective is to stop seeing social media as a painful slog. Instead, she wants her clients to view it as a chance for warm conversation with people they care about. (One slide declares, "How 'I hate social media' Is Hurting You." Another shows four ways to start a conversation as if you were on a coffee date.)

No matter what you're creating—a newsletter article, podcast episode, blog post, event, course, or signature talk—your goal isn't to teach people everything you know, so resist the urge to cram in as much as possible. Your number of learning objectives can vary, but as a starting

**A transformative talk isn't about imparting knowledge.** It's about empowering your people to do something differently in their life or work.

point, try limiting yourself to three for every section. As you develop your outline, see if that practice helps you avoid overthinking your content. Karnes's talk has three sections: mindset, action plan, and implementation.

## Share What Lights You Up

This isn't the first time I've asked you to tell your story. It's so important! Whenever I facilitate a learning experience, those who approach me afterward say something about my stories and mission. Don't get so caught up in information that you forget to share *why* your content matters to you. Karnes knew speaking would be good for business, but developing her talks helped her determine how to connect with the right audience for her programs. "When I first started, I knew a way to attract leads—a good place for me to be—was on stage. Using signature talks has organized my thoughts and built my confidence. I feel empowered to be in front of the room sharing my stories and connecting with my clients, and that has opened so many doors for me."

Any time you share your story, it's never about you. It's always about your people. To illustrate your unique mission, share your vulnerability but also give your audience strategies for making their own lives better. Do whatever you can to weave in references to them. The more specific you can be about their struggles, circumstances, and dreams, the better.

Karnes's social media talk describes a point in her entrepreneurial journey where she felt stuck. One way she emerged out of her funk was by committing to posting about her business experiences every day for six months. "I had to let go of perfect and share what lights me up," she says. Over time, her following grew. But as she explains, the growing likes didn't provide clarity and confidence—the dialogues she was leading did. As she shared her fears, vulnerabilities, and deepest ambitions, she started attracting the kind of ambitious seekers she now serves through her community-driven business model.

## Interact with Your Audience

Once you've chosen the best container to teach your thing, build space for your people to share their ideas, with you and especially with each other. Even if you're giving a talk and your time slot is just ten minutes, you can poll them or ask for a single volunteer. Don't let the opportunity to listen to your people pass you by. You can always learn something valuable that will inform your work.

Like me, Karnes adapts her talks to a variety of audiences. The longer the time she has, the more interaction she facilitates. Her unique methodology combines her ebullient personality with her IT-driven systems background. One way she helps busy entrepreneurs lighten the load of social media is to create a chart that lays out topics and themes. In long versions of her talk, she builds in time for attendees to fill in the chart with their own themes, complete with a worksheet. She then coaches the group in how to translate these themes into posts. For shorter versions where there's not time for an activity, she might ask for one volunteer to share. Either way, Karnes knows there's value in letting her people talk. No matter what kind of learning experience you create, make room to do the same.

## Provide an Action Step for Working with You

If you've been trained not to take up space or if you feel squeamish about self-promotion, you may be vulnerable to the trap of not making an ask. My rule is that while events, content pieces, and learning experiences are *not* a pitch, I provide next steps for connecting with me.

Even if you don't want to promote a service or an offering, you should include something specific for people to act on. For example, I've gleaned valuable information by bringing half sheets to workshops I lead, with checklists for participants to indicate interest in future programs. Some attendees may want to work with you, so let them know exactly how. Keep it short and easy to understand. When in doubt, reach out to an event's organizer with questions or ideas. For example, they may forbid speakers to sell during the session, but will allow you to set up a table during a break or at a vendor booth.

Karnes's programming has since expanded, but her first offer was a social media bootcamp. When seeking her initial participants, she used her talk as her primary marketing tool. At the time, she delivered it to a professional speaking group she was part of. "I got three clients out of just one presentation there," she says. Later that year, she repeated the talk to another group. In the audience was one of her existing clients who'd seen the talk before. But this time, it inspired her to go even further with Karnes, signing up for one of her higher-ticket offerings.

Maybe you're like Karnes and know deep down you need to be in front of a room. Or maybe your thing right now isn't a signature talk, but rather a blog, podcast, event, or cohort program. Regardless of how you choose to go about it, I implore you to claim full ownership of your value as a big-hearted entrepreneur.

Take what's unique about you, your business, and your mission, and amplify it far and wide in just the way your people need to hear it. May your business be a tool for gathering them together in a dialogue that brings the change you wish to see in your neighborhood, your community, or the world.

### ⑦ REFLECT

- What are the top three learning objectives that can propel your people to improve their life or work?

- What idea, system, or common status quo practice are you taking a stand against, and how can your story show why you care about it?

- What method (or methods) do you want to use to amplify a mission that matters—newsletter, blog, podcast, event, group program, signature talk?

- Experiment with some hooks that could grab your audience in the first thirty seconds of your chosen method.

- What do you want your audience to see differently at the end of your content or program?

- What kind of audience interaction might your experience include?

- What next step will you invite your audience to take?

## ☆ MAKE IT PRETTY

You researched and played around with software after reading the last chapter, right? Now, design some slides! No matter what kind of container you want to build for learning, slides are an effective tool for arranging your ideas. Identify the action steps, or learning objectives, that can propel your people the most. Then, bring the content to life visually. Bring in your brand colors, photos that illustrate your story, and infographics or other images that remind your people that you relate to their pain points and aspirations.

## ♡ BRING IT TO LIFE

Outline a content piece or learning experience. On a single sheet, write short sentences on each of the following prompts:

- Your hook
- Your learning objectives (start with three and go from there). For each one, complete this sentence: "After this experience, participants will be able to..."
- Stories that illustrate your learning objectives
- Audience interaction
- Next step for working with you

# Loving Disruptors, May You Never Feel Alone

To ALL the loving disruptors, may you never feel alone. As you continue your journey of bringing humanity to business, my big-hearted mentors, peers, and clients are here to cheer you on. The final question of my interviews was, "Is there anything related to big-hearted entrepreneurship I didn't ask that you want my readers to know?" Here are abbreviated versions of some of their responses.

**Algernon Hall:** "Keep your eyes on the mission."

**Angele Goss:** "It's not the money that moves you along, so there has to be something about it that you really enjoy and could spend endless hours doing."

**Anne Ingersoll:** "If you have an idea that you really believe in, there's a way to make it into a business while finding joy and putting your mission into the world. Surround yourself with the right people, and be resilient when you're faced with obstacles."

**Barb Buckner Suárez:** "There are more of us than you think!"

**Bethany Hegedus:** "With each phase, both you and your mission grow and deepen. To keep investing in yourself as well as the business takes courage. Seek community, find folks you trust, cultivate relationships. Do not run yourself into the ground. There is nothing big-hearted in the typical grind culture way of working."

**Calvin Koon-Stack:** "No matter what you charge, your time has value. That's true regardless of whether you're just starting out or have years of business experience behind you. Respecting that value sometimes means saying no to new projects, or choosing to spend it on yourself or your family. Embracing that can be a *win* bigger than any deal."

**Cindy Karnes:** "Release the guilt and shame about not doing enough. Pay attention to what's out of alignment. Keep at it, and when things are in alignment, you are unstoppable."

**Jason Jones:** "Mission-driven entrepreneurs need to get right with their relationship with money. The bigger the impact you have, the more you will sell, which will provide you with resources to make a bigger impact. Work on being a good and open receiver of financial success and it will amplify your impact."

**Kate Stower:** "Talk to each other in person (and be sure to include food)! Maybe a beer, maybe a cup of coffee, but sit down and look people in the eye and have a conversation. It's a powerful experience connecting with another human being."

Here's to owning your worth, amplifying your mission, **and becoming unstoppable!**

**Laina Latterner:** "Make sure people feel educated enough to form their own opinion. Knowledge is power. Once you know a little bit of something, it connects to something else and impacts everything."

**Liz Dempsey Lee:** "If there's one thing I wish someone had said to me, it would be to trust yourself to start. If you have that feeling that you don't know how to implement your ideas or that they are risky or different, think about what's blocking you. Take just one step forward and see where that takes you."

**Matthew Cibellis:** "Don't be afraid to show clients 'the mission is great, but you matter.' The more humanity you bring, the more effective your projects will be."

**Mindy Martell:** "Build a solid support network around you."

**Shona Ramchandani:** "Give yourself permission to own your worth!"

**Whitney Brimfield:** "Relationship building and relationship maintenance are some of your biggest jobs as an entrepreneur."

Here's to owning your worth, amplifying your mission, and becoming unstoppable!

# Acknowledgements

To JENNIFER SLY, my visionary friend who foresaw this book before I did. I'll be forever grateful for your spookily astute insights like, "Why don't you take some time in New Mexico and write your book?"

To my partner, Fred Woltman, for calmly hanging by on the many days and evenings I skipped fun things to write, and for reminding me, "when all feels lost... shower!"

To the crew at Authors Who Lead, who facilitated the cohort where I wrote my original manuscript: Azul Terronez for teaching us what becoming an author really means; Steve Vannoy, Heather Dyer, and Amanda Toynbee for holding space while it came to be; Sybil Hall, whose book came out at the same time as mine (eee!), may your education wisdom traverse the globe; and Carmin Caterina and Lucy Rivera for sharing your stories as we created together.

To my entrepreneur pals Nancy Burger, Angele Goss, Bethany Hegedus, Anne Ingersoll, Ivy Kaminksy, and Brooke Lancaster: I couldn't ask for a better collection of ride-or-dies, and I can't wait to see where our journeys take us together.

To the women whose dinners, walks, and calls remind me who I am and make everything better: Katie Brown, Melissa Burkhart, Jessica Hackner, Amy Lovaas, Shannon Pennefeather, Kate Stower, and Ellen Tuthill.

To the Page Two Team for bringing this big-hearted vision to life: Jesse Finkelstein for seeing I had this book inside me; Kendra Ward for her keen editorial eye, calm nudges, insightful questions, and surgeon-quality cuts; Taysia Louie for capturing the book's soul through her artistic style; Madison Taylor, whose glorious style sheet brought a tear to this former copy editor's eye; Adrineh Der-Boghossian for keeping everything on track while helping the journey feel light; Meghan O'Neill and Ariel Hudnall for trusting me with their cohort vision and teaching me the ropes of author outreach; Indu Singh for eagle-eyed proofing; and Leonni Antono for her vibrant marketing imagery.

To Jeffrey Davis for showing me what business artistry looks like.

To the mentors, peers, and clients who shared their stories and turned this project from a "me" into a "we": Whitney Brimfield, Barb Buckner Suárez, Matthew Cibellis, Molly Clark, Cassandra Davis Speed, Liz Dempsey Lee, Algernon Hall, Jason Jones, Cindy Karnes, Calvin Koon-Stack, Laina Latterner, Maddy Kaudy, Mindy Martell, and Shona Ramchandani.

And to mom and dad for showing Michael and me what it means to be public servants, modeling a can-do spirit for life, and believing in this project from the start.

# Bibliography

Abrams, Stacey. *Lead from the Outside: How to Build Your Future and Make Real Change.* New York: Picador, 2018.

Carter, Kristoffer. *Permission to Glow: A Spiritual Guide to Epic Leadership.* Vancouver: Page Two Books, 2021.

Clark, Dorie. *Entrepreneurial You: Monetize Your Expertise, Create Multiple Income Streams, and Thrive.* Boston: Harvard Business Review Press, 2017.

Fata, Mike. *Grow: 12 Unconventional Lessons for Becoming an Unstoppable Entrepreneur.* Vancouver: Page Two Books, 2023.

Fields, Jonathan. *Sparked: Discover Your Unique Imprint for Work that Makes You Come Alive.* New York: HarperCollins Leadership, 2021.

Gerasimo, Pilar. *The Healthy Deviant: A Rule Breaker's Guide to Being Healthy in an Unhealthy World.* Berkeley: North Atlantic Books, 2020.

Hendricks, Gay. *The Joy of Genius: The Next Step Beyond The Big Leap.* Cardiff: Waterside Productions, 2018.

Hogshead, Sally. *How the World Sees You: Discover Your Highest Value Through the Science of Fascination.* New York: Harper Business, 2014.

Hurst, Aaron. *The Purpose Economy: How Your Desire for Impact, Personal Growth and Community Is Changing the World.* Boise: Elevate, 2016.

Jarvis, Paul. *Company of One: Why Staying Small Is the Next Big Thing for Business*. Boston: Mariner Books, 2019.

Kane, Christine. *The Soul-Sourced Entrepreneur: An Unconventional Success Plan for the Highly Creative, Secretly Sensitive & Wildly Ambitious*. Dallas: BenBella Books, 2020.

Kleon, Austin. *Show Your Work! 10 Ways to Share Your Creativity and Get Discovered*. New York: Workman Publishing, 2014.

Lavingia, Sahil. *The Minimalist Entrepreneur: How Great Founders Do More with Less*. New York: Portfolio/Penguin, 2021.

Loy, Alice, and Tom Aageson. *Creative Economy Entrepreneurs: From Startup to Success: How Entrepreneurs in the Creative Industries Are Transforming the Global Economy*. Santa Fe: Creative Startups, 2018.

Luna, Elle. *The Crossroads of Should and Must: Find and Follow Your Passion*. New York: Workman Publishing Company, 2015.

McKeown, Greg. *Essentialism: The Disciplined Pursuit of Less*. New York: Crown Publishing, 2014.

Mohr, Tara. *Playing Big: Practical Wisdom for Women Who Want to Speak Up, Create, and Lead*. New York: Avery, 2014.

Mulcahy, Diane. *The Gig Economy: The Complete Guide to Getting Better Work, Taking More Time Off, and Financing the Life You Want!* New York: American Management Association, 2017.

Napper, Paul, and Anthony Rao. *The Power of Agency: The 7 Principles to Conquer Obstacles, Make Effective Decisions & Create a Life on Your Own Terms*. New York: St. Martin's Press, 2019.

Palmer, Kimberly. *The Economy of You: Discover Your Inner Entrepreneur and Recession-Proof Your Life*. New York: American Management Association, 2014.

Parker, Priya. *The Art of Gathering: How We Meet and Why It Matters*. New York: Riverhead Books, 2018.

Rimington, Jess, and Joanna Levitt Cea. *Beloved Economies: Transforming How We Work*. Vancouver: Page Two Books, 2022.

Rodgers, Rachel. *We Should All Be Millionaires: A Woman's Guide to Earning More, Building Wealth and Gaining Economic Power*. Nashville: HarperCollins Leadership, 2021.

Savoia, Alberto. *The Right It: Why So Many Ideas Fail and How to Make Sure Yours Succeed*. New York: HarperOne, 2019.

Sincero, Jen. *You Are a Badass at Making Money: Master the Mindset of Wealth*. New York: Penguin Life, 2017.

Slim, Pamela. *Body of Work: Finding the Thread That Ties Your Story Together*. New York: Portfolio, 2013.

Sonora Beam, Lisa. *The Creative Entrepreneur: A DIY Visual Guidebook for Making Business Ideas Real*. Beverly: Quarry Books, 2008.

Taulbert, Clifton L., and Gary Schoeniger. *Who Owns the Ice House? Eight Life Lessons from an Unlikely Entrepreneur*. Washington: ELI Press, 2010.

Tawwab, Nedra Glover. *Set Boundaries, Find Peace: A Guide to Reclaiming Yourself*. New York: TarcherPerigee, 2021.

Trent, Tererai. *The Awakened Woman: Remembering and Reigniting Our Sacred Dreams*. New York: Atra/Enliven Books, 2017.

Villanueva, Edgar. *Decolonizing Wealth: Indigenous Wisdom to Heal Divides and Restore Balance*. Oakland: Berrett-Koehler, 2021.

Wilding, Melody. *Trust Yourself: Stop Overthinking and Channel Your Emotions for Success at Work*. San Francisco: Prism, 2021.

PHOTO: BELÉN FLEMING

# About the Author

**SUZI HUNN** founded Teach Your Thing in 2017 to help changemakers amplify their impact. Her specialty is designing education experiences that expand audiences and create income streams.

Entrepreneurship can be a powerful tool for bringing humanity to our world of work. She is committed to facilitating dialogue about making this happen.

Suzi has more than twenty years' experience developing learning tools for nonprofits, social enterprises, cultural institutions, K–12 schools, corporate groups, authors, and founders. As an educator at the Minnesota Historical Society, her largest project was coordinating the second edition of *Northern Lights*, a history curriculum used by sixty-five thousand sixth graders annually. Other favorites included multimedia materials on Ojibwe beadwork and Hmong immigration, and presenting at conferences like Games+Learning+Society and National Council for the Social Studies.

She lives by the rallying cry, "You have medicine that you must own." Suzi lives in Minneapolis–St. Paul with her partner and golden retriever.

# LET'S KEEP THE CONVERSATION GOING 🩶

**I LOVE TALKING ABOUT BIG-HEARTED ENTREPRENEURSHIP!** Let's chat about empowering people through teaching what you know. Feel free to reach out with questions or ideas. I look forward to hearing from you.

## Invite Me to Speak

If your social enterprise, nonprofit, or event would benefit from a talk or workshop on big-hearted entrepreneurship or learning design, reach out and see if we're a good fit. Fill out the contact form on my website or request a chat through social media.

## Share Your Thoughts for Future Readers

Did reading *Big-Hearted Entrepreneur* inspire you or your work? If so, I'd love to hear about it. And if you think these stories and ideas might help others, I invite you to leave a positive review on your favorite online bookseller or reading community. It would help spread the word, and I'd be forever grateful!

## Reach Out with Questions or Ideas

Connecting with inspired people is one of my favorite parts of running a business. If there's something burning you'd like to share with me, give yourself permission to reach out (find me on social media or fill out the contact form on my website). We can't do this work alone, and I'm curious to hear about the questions, solutions, or collaborations cooking in your mind.

## Subscribe to My Newsletter

If you want to hear the latest from Teach Your Thing, visit my website to sign up for email updates on education content and big-hearted entrepreneurship.

teachyourthing.com

Teach Your Thing

www.ingramcontent.com/pod-product-compliance
Lightning Source LLC
Chambersburg PA
CBHW031104080526
44587CB00011B/822